THE ART OF GOD

The Making of Christians and the Meaning of Worship

Christopher Irvine

First published in Great Britain in 2005.
Society for Promoting Christian Knowledge 36 Causton Street
London SW1P 4AU

Mary Fox was the production editor. The design is by Anna Manhart. Cover image: *The Hand of God,* by Auguste Rodin. It has been provided courtesy of The Metropolitan Museum of Art, Gift of Edward D. Adams, 1908 (08.210) Photograph © 1978 The Metropolitan Museum of Art. The typesetting was done by Kari Nicholls. The index was compiled by Kris Fankhouser and Mary Fox.

Printed in the United States of America.

Library of Congress Control Number 2006924861

ISBN-10: 1-56854-250-X
ISBN-13: 978-1-56854-250-8

ARTGOD

For Rosie, Beth, Ruth, Luke and Benjamin,
with love and gratitude

Contents

List of Figures and Illustrations

Figures

Illustrations

Acknowledgments

I am indebted to a number of friends and colleagues whose support and interest have contributed significantly to the writing of this book. I am especially grateful to Professor Paul Bradshaw for suggesting that I should write on this topic. It began with a paper entitled "Liturgical Celebration and Formation: Some Work in Progress" delivered to the Society for Liturgical Study at Mirfield in August 2002. I am particularly grateful to Bridget Nichols for her interest in the topic, and for her helpful comments and suggestions as I embarked on a further project, an analysis of formational language in contemporary liturgical revision, which was presented to a meeting of the International Anglican Liturgical Consultation in Oxford in August 2003. The book that has emerged is far broader in scope than my two research projects. I am grateful to David Hebblethwaite, a former secretary of the Church of England Liturgical Commission, for his assistance in researching an aspect of the history of the compilation of *The Alternative Service Book 1980.* I am also indebted to Benedict Green, CR, for kindly reading the first full draft version of the manuscript. His learned eye spotted a number of errors, but I must take full responsibility for those that remain.

A number of modern poets are cited in Chapter 3, and I am grateful to the following publishers and copyright holders for allowing me to cite from their work. The work of Denise Levertov, published by Bloodaxe Books, is reproduced by permission of Pollinger Limited and the proprietor. Bloodaxe Books have also granted permission to quote from Christiania Whitehead's poem "Deer at Dawn," from her collection *The Garden of Slender Trust* (Bloodaxe Books Ltd, 1999). David Higham Associates have granted permission to cite the work of Elizabeth Jennings and Louis MacNeice. The publishers Faber & Faber Ltd have granted permission for me to cite a line from Seamus Heaney's poem "Seeing Things," from his collection *Seeing Things* (Faber & Faber Limited, 1991). I must also thank Anne Stevenson for her kindness in allowing me to freely quote from her work published in *The Collected Poems* (Bloodaxe Books Ltd, 2002). The biblical quotations are generally from the New Revised Standard Version (Oxford University Press, 1995); those marked with an asterisk are my own translation.

I must also express my thanks to the staff and students of the College of the Resurrection, Mirfield, for their patience and kindly support. I was granted a term's study leave by the College in the summer term of 2004, and gained much from the hospitality and worship of the Benedictine Abbey of Saint Matthias in Trier, Germany. As always, conversations were integral to the whole process of writing, and thanks must be expressed to Mark Oakley, Peter Allan, CR, Phil Ritchie, Thomas Seville, CR, and David Neaum for their interest and helpful comments. I must note, too, my thanks to George Guiver, CR, for his constant support and particularly for his assistance with the illustrations, and to Hope Greene, who photographed the illustrations of the Ravenna mosaics that appear on pages 102 and 114. Last, but by no means least, I must thank my immediate family, Rosie, Beth, Ruth and Luke, to whom I dedicate this book.

Christopher Irvine

Introduction

You must change your life.

Rainer Maria Rilke

Every book has a history, and the origin of this book lies in two points I made in *Art and Worship* (Dawtry and Irvine, 2002), that we ourselves are God's art, his making, and that we might view the place where Christians gather and invoke the name of the Trinity as being God's studio. Christians, we are told, are made and not born (Tertullian), and the thesis of this book is that our being made Christian is the very meaning of worship. It is, I believe, the regular joining with others in prayer, and especially in the celebration of the Eucharist, that is the making of a Christian. The poet and artist David Jones memorably demonstrated the inseparable link between art and sacrament, while my own search for a language to speak of liturgical formation has led me to a deeper appreciation and exploration of art and of the Christian understanding of what it is to be and to become a person in community with others.

What has emerged from my reading and reflection is a work of liturgical theology, an attempt to elucidate the meaning of worship as the making of Christians. The book falls into two parts: the first explores the theological sources and resources from which we might draw this understanding of Christian liturgy; the second looks specifically at the formative effect of worship on its participants, particularly in sacramental celebration. In terms of the sequence and subject matter of the six main chapters, the book mirrors that of the Christian liturgy, with its two-fold structure of Word and Sacrament. The first three chapters present the Word, that is, God's call (which we might hear as "vocation") to become what he is seeking to make of us. Chapters 4 to 6 seek to elucidate an understanding of how this might happen through our participation in worship, specifically in the celebration of Baptism and the Eucharist.

As the book began to take shape, I realized that the issues and questions my exploration raised coincided with some of the most pressing challenges facing traditional Western Christianity. As Anthony

Giddens has shown in *Modernity and Self-Identity* (1991), the question, "Who am I?" is one of the focal quandaries for people living in late modernity. It is this question that runs like a thread and gives a thematic coherence to the specific conundrum treated in the book. In one sense, the conundrum of who we are relates to the question "To whom do we belong?" but finally, the question can only be answered in terms of the vision of what it is that we believe God is calling us to be. Having made us in the divine image, God seeks to shape us into the likeness of his Son, Jesus Christ. Thus the first chapter of the book addresses the question of who we are in the visual terms of our being made "in the image and according to the likeness of God." Chapter 2 traces out the New Testament witness to Christ as the pattern of what it is that God is calling us to be and become as Christians. But this survey of the New Testament yields something more, a vision of Christianity as a religion of transformation, change and transfiguration. It is this vision that casts light upon the meaning of worship, and for this reason, the book begins not with a discussion of worship, but an outline of that vision as it is shown in Christian art and witnessed to in Scripture and Christian theological reflection. The book is liberally peppered with biblical references: the reader is urged to track these passages in their Bible and to take time in pondering the words of Scripture. Similarly I hope that the references I make to artists, paintings, poetry, and sculpture will act as a springboard for the reader to extend their appreciation of these artists and their works. The Internet, of course, is a wonderful means of viewing art and of discovering more about artists and their works. The very accessibility of art in our digital age is not without its downside however. In a culture saturated with images, artistic and electronic, how is the vision of Christianity as a religion of transformation to be recognized? How are we literally to be "see-ers," those who recognize the epiphanies of God? In Chapter 3, I draw upon the work and vocation of the poet, as a type of seer, as one who is searching and straining to find the language to signal the transforming presence of the transcendent in our world and in human lives. The discussion of poetry leads into a consideration of the sung poetry of the Church, its hymnody, and gives special attention to Charles Wesley's vision of God refashioning us to his design through the Spirit. Underlying Chapter 4 is an analysis of the language of contemporary worship, and here I attempt to show that the best language of corporate worship is spun from the biblical images of our being made and made new in Christ and through the Spirit. If the primary effect of worship is, as this central chapter seeks to demonstrate, the formation of worshippers into the likeness of Christ, then the emphasis we place on what we do in worship has to be balanced with a sense of what we receive in worship. Our active participation in worship has to be matched, in other words, with an openness to being fully engaged by the reality of the mystery of God. And if we are to be grasped by the vision of God shaping us into the image of his beloved Son, within his corporate body, the Church, then our approach to worship might well need to change. This leads to an appeal for a recovery of a more contemplative approach both to worship and to the ways in which we reflect upon God. Such a contemplative view is presupposed in the visionary texts of the Scriptures, in both the Old and New Testaments, which testify to the transforming effect of our being encountered by the mystery of God.

As the question of who we are and what we are called to become is played out in the successive chapters of the book, we meet another key problem of modern thought, the question of our embodied existence, and our cultural preoccupation with the body. Fergus Kerr, in what must surely qualify as a classic theological exposition of the philosophical questions of human identity, *Theology after Wittgenstein* (1986), has shown that the conventional way we speak of the human body and soul lures us mistakenly to imagine that we might discover the soul when we peel back the layers of flesh. The procedure, as he wryly observes, is rather like peeling the skins of an onion. In the end there is nothing left but the layers of skin. But as the tradition of the healing miracles in the Gospels attests, the physical body is also the focus of the Christian enterprise, and the point has received particular treatment in recent theological writing, not least in that of feminist writers, of whom we might cite Elisabeth Moltmann-Wendel, and the telling title of her book *I am My Body* (1994). Resources for understanding this key contemporary question of human embodiment are found in the sources I cite in Chapter 1 and, indeed, provide the basis on which I set out the essentially embodied activity of Christian worship in Chapters 5 and 6.

As one eminent liturgical scholar, John Baldovin (1996, p. 132), emphatically says, "disembodied worship is merely a figment of the imagination." I suggest that the primacy of liturgy as embodied action might well provide a way of addressing one of the most pressing theological questions as to how Western Christians might find ways of understanding and communicating to others, living in the conditions of late modernity, the meaning of baptism and the Eucharist. It has been said that our time is marked by a "crisis of sacramentality," and that this crisis lies at the roots of the serious decline of traditional European Christianity. It could be that the vision of Christianity as a transformational religion, which I attempt to trace from the sources and resources of theological reflection, might well provide an open window through which we might see and catch a sense of what it is to live in a sacramental world. In addition, the understanding of sacramental celebration as being a bodily transaction might again provide a productive point of dialogue with modern and postmodern cultural reflection on personal identity and social meaning.

The thought that sacramental action is transacted in and through the body occurred to me during a celebration of the Eucharist at the Benedictine Abbey of Saint Matthias in Trier. It was one of those unsought and spontaneous moments of recognition. The community and members of the congregation were gathered in a horseshoe around a free-standing altar in the choir of this great Romanesque abbey church. The priest who had presided was about to administer Communion to the assistants, and it suddenly occurred to me that the altar was directly above the tombs of the first two bishops of the Roman city of Trier, Eucharius and Valerius, in the crypt directly below. And there we were, gathered together to receive the sacramental Body of Christ. What dawned upon me at that particular moment was the existence of a layering of bodies. Buried in the crypt were the bodies of the first two bishops representing, as it were, the earliest stratum of the Christian Church in that place; above the crypt the contemporary Church was gathered, a part of the universal Body of Christ, to receive the sacrament of Christ's Body from the altar around which we had gathered. This disparate group of people, these bodies, were called to become one body, through their participation in the sacrament. Through the receiving of this inestimable gift of Communion, Christ sought to be embodied in each of the communicants, for as Hilary, the fourth-century Bishop of Poitiers exclaimed, through sharing in the holy mysteries and receiving the holy gift of Communion, Christ shall be in us, and we in Christ. The answer to the question of who I am is written out in the interactions between ourselves and others, but if we allow ourselves to become God's art, his making, then we know that we ourselves can be Christ for each other.

The epilogue, Chapter 7, is deliberately reflective and invites the reader to contemplate two images of formation by the sculptor Auguste Rodin. As we contemplate these two images in the light of God's art, we might well be moved to reciprocate the risk God takes of placing himself in our hands, and trustingly place ourselves, and those whose lives are bound up with ours, into the hands of God, which is the movement of prayer, and itself a creative act of love.

1

Whose Image and Likeness?

The question "whose image and likeness?" like a good number of searching questions, was forged in the heat of controversy and disagreement. A group of Pharisees and some of Herod's party approached Jesus and asked him if it were lawful to pay taxes to Caesar. Jesus responded, as he sometimes did, by posing a counter-question. He called for a coin and asked: "Whose likeness and inscription is this?" "Caesar's," they replied, and with impeccable logic Jesus confounded his opponents by saying, "Render to Caesar the things that belong to Caesar and to God the things that belong to God." (Mark 12:13–17; Matthew 22:5–22; Luke 20:20–26). On this occasion Jesus effectively silenced his opponents, but the well-known saying leaves us with a tantalizing question. The coin bore the image of the Roman emperor, but who or what is it that bears the stamp of God? To rephrase the question, we might ask where we might see the imprint of God, and how we too might come to recognize and return what "belongs to God."

The witness of Scripture is that the whole world is of God's making, fashioned by his own hands: "The sea is his, for he made it, and his hands have molded the dry land" (Psalm 95:5). It is God's creation, and as the whole natural order, with its variety and kaleidoscope of color and form, belongs to God: "The earth is the Lord's and all that fills it" (Psalm 24:1); so all that we might offer to God comes from the rich resource of his own making: "all things come from you, and of your own do we give you" (see 1 Chronicles 29:10b–13). In this there is much we might say about our stewardship of natural resources, our management, as it were, of the divine economy. But what concerns us here is first this sense of the natural world having been made, of it being there, of it literally being before us and existing independently of us. It is the sense of the external natural world, and beyond it to the whole exploding cosmos with its myriad galaxies and immeasurable distances of interstellar space, being given and shown to us rather as an artist might exhibit his or her work. Basil of Caesarea (c. 330–379), who is regarded as one of the founding fathers of Eastern Christianity, once described the created world as "God's studio," and even the austere Continental Reformer, John Calvin, who regarded religion and art as a dangerous mix, designated the created world as "the theatre of God's glory." The use of artistic analogies by such key theological writers is very telling, and opens up a fruitful dialogue between our attempts to speak of the creator God and the artist's endeavor of making art. There is considerable common ground covering areas of creativity, but there is something even more fundamental about the very fact of the world, of it simply being there, existing in the reality of its physicality quite apart from the perceiving human subject.

In this respect we might consider the work of the artist Paul Cézanne (1839–1906), who having taken his leave from the Impressionists with their preoccupation with the perceiving human subject, sought painterly ways of showing the world in its givenness. As he embarked on his artistic path Cézanne admitted to his lifelong friend, the French novelist Emile Zola, that nature presented him with the greatest difficulties. But what he achieved in his still-life paintings was a way of depicting an object in its "thereness"(rather than arranged according to some aesthetic convention), and thereby he brought to light that most basic presupposition of the Christian doctrine of creation, namely the distinction between the Creator and creation and the sense of creation as given, as gift. Further, it is this sheer gratuitous quality and the objective givenness of creation that opens the possibility of God's self-communication to us sacramentally, that is through the medium of physical matter and in a manner that meets our nature as sensible creatures, as those who come to know anything or anyone, primarily through sight, sound, taste, smell and touch. Creation is, we might say, the necessary presupposition of a sacramental universe.

But this is to race ahead and anticipate the line of our argument. Returning to Cézanne, we might consider his still-life paintings, such as *Still Life with Apples and Oranges* painted around 1899. It is a symphony of color, and depicts a selection of fruit placed on a table covered with two richly patterned cloths. A plate of apples, oranges in a compotier, other fruits and a jug rest on a white tablecloth and zigzag of drapery that falls away in two directions from the front edge of the table. It is as though what was there before the painter had been "revealed," literally unveiled and shown in the particularity of its existence, in the specificity of its givenness, in its singular coloring and texture. As Picasso once said, "I don't seek, I find"; the world is gratuitous, it is simply there, and there to be discovered and delighted in.

Consider again Cézanne's painting *Five Bathers* (1877–1878). This small painted panel might well be viewed as a celebration of creation. The composition is of naked human forms on a riverbank, recalling the Paradise that in the biblical myth is located by reference to the four rivers. The voluptuous flesh of the bathers set in a luscious verdant setting evokes a sense of beings fecund and fully alive, recalling that note of divine exuberance in the biblical hymn of creation: "And God blessed them, and said to them, 'Be fruitful and multiply, and fill the earth'" (Genesis 1:28). Cézanne's bathers are painted in different postures; the dynamic composition suggests a kind of dance, a celebration of the created natural order. So what we see in this painting is an icon of God's good creation, given to us in all its material physicality for our delight and for our flourishing. As we begin to draw an answer to the question of what it might mean to "render to God the things that are God's" we could say that it is, in part, a recognition of the "givenness" of the natural world and of our human capacity to wonder and delight in a cosmos that bears the very signature of God.

But let us return to the story with which we began, the story of Jesus' encounter with the Pharisees, and, with a flick of the coin, ask again: "Whose image and likeness is this?" The language is ambiguous, perhaps deliberately so, and leads us to wonder where we might trace the image of God. The irony is that although the story leads us to place Caesar and God as polar opposites, even Caesar bears the imprint of God's making, for he too, despite the adornments of imperial power, is made in the image of God.

So where is this "image of God" to be located and seen? The question invites us to explore the wisdom of the Christian tradition, to dig down to the very foundations of this particular Christian doctrine that seeks to articulate the mystery of what it is to be and become a human being. From earliest times in the history of Christian reflection there has been a tendency to associate the image of God, the *imago Dei,* with some superior or higher human faculty. Thus, for instance, the third-century Origen of Alexandria, working within the categories of Greek

Platonic philosophy, equated the divine image with what in Greek was termed the *nous*—what we would call the human mind. In part, the locating of the true image of God in the rational, inward soul of the individual was a reaction against the danger of idolatry, strictly denounced in Scripture, and a strategy to distance Christianity from the plethora of artistic images adorning the temples of the largely pagan environment in which Christians at that time found themselves (see Origen, *Against Celsus* VII.66). Consequently, the more Christians reflected on this doctrine of humankind—created *imago Dei,* the further they retreated from the pictorial and the very physicality of human existence.

In the history of Western Christianity, the parameters in the debate on the nature of the human person were definitively drawn by Augustine of Hippo (354–430). Augustine was the apostle of inwardness and charted the inner mental landscape of the human person. He was compelled to seek after God, and his subject was the human soul, which he incisively analyzed with unparalleled sophistication. In his series of commentaries on Genesis, Augustine notes how God says in the first creation story, "Let *us* make humankind in *our* image," and interprets these plural prepositions as a code for the triunal God, revealed in Christian experience as a trinity of mutual love, with the Father as the eternal lover, the Son, Jesus Christ, as the beloved, and the Holy Spirit the very bond of love. Augustine saw this same trinity mirrored in the human soul. The *imago Dei* became the *imago trinitatis,* but this was emphatically located in the soul. In each of his three commentaries on the creation stories of Genesis, Augustine pointed to the "innermost and principal element" of the interior man, where "reason and intelligence is to be found." But the image had been darkened and deformed by human sin, if not, as his earlier writings suggested, totally obliterated. The true image of God was Christ: the Christian, as a creature endowed with reason, could, by God's grace, participate in the divine wisdom and grow into the likeness of Christ by coming to see and act in the world in accordance with God's gentle and generous ways.

The later Augustine, in speaking of the baptized participating in the life of God, came close to the Eastern doctrine of deification, and almost reiterated Athanasius in suggesting that the incarnation was God's redemptive act and the very basis of our salvation: for "joining to us the likeness of His humanity, he took away the unlikeness of our iniquity; and having been made a partaker of our mortality, made us partakers of his divinity" (*De Trinitate* IV.2, 4). But again, such participation was seen to belong to the region of the "inner man," which Augustine identified with the highest human faculty of the mind. Taking his cue from the Letter to the Ephesians which exhorts its readers to be "renewed in the spirit of your minds" (Ephesians 4:23; cf. Romans 12:2 and Colossians 3:9), Augustine could only speak of a rather uncertain and lifelong transformation of the inner human being," deferring any sense of the transformation of the body to the resurrection on the last day of divine judgment. So it was not the physical representable form, but the human mind that imaged God. Indeed, Augustine went so far as to say that the mind, with its triad of "memory, will, and understanding," provided the best analogy of the divine trinity, Father, Son and Holy Spirit.

In locating the *imago Dei* in the inner rational mind, how then did Augustine view the physical human body? There is an undeniable ambivalence in Augustine's references to the body; it was to be loved, but frequently needed to be rebuked, checked and controlled. As Peter Brown demonstrates in his magisterial book *The Body and Society* (1989), Augustine's view of the body was not entirely negative. The physical body was regarded as a constituent part of human nature. Indeed, Augustine offers the view that before the Fall and their expulsion from the garden of Paradise, Adam and Eve had known a perfect harmony and balance between body and soul. Indeed, the painful rupturing of soul and body was the dreaded pain experienced by Christians at the moment of death. Augustine recognized that the body of the baptized Christian was "a temple of the Holy Spirit" (1 Corinthians 6:19), and for this reason he insisted that even the dead corpse of the Christian man and woman had to be approached and handled with reverence.

The typical understanding of humankind as the image of God in Eastern Christianity is built upon the view of Irenaeus (c. 130–c. 200), the influential teacher and Bishop of Lyons, who drew a crucial distinction between "image" and "likeness." The earliest teachers of Christianity drew from the Septuagint, the Greek translation of the Old Testament, in which the terms "image" and "likeness" in Genesis 5:1–26 were translated by the terms *eikon* for image and *homoiosis* for likeness, which rather exaggerated the difference in meaning between the two terms.

Irenaeus of Lyons, and later Origen, took the word "image" to be a dynamic term and one which spoke of potentiality: God had created humankind with the capacity to grow into the likeness of God. Origen was more speculative in his approach: taking his cue from the fact that there are two creation stories in the Book of Genesis he suggested that there was a double creation, first a spiritual creation and then a physical and material making of the cosmos. Irenaeus rejected this double creation, but argued, on the basis that humankind, both male and female, was made *in* the image of God and *after* God's likeness, that Adam and Eve had not in fact grown to maturity. They were made in the image, but had not attained the likeness of God.

True human maturity, the goal of being made in the image of God, was to grow into the likeness of God. This was conceived as the goal of creation, the consummation of God's creative (and recreative) work in Christ. It received a particular emphasis in the theology of the seventh-century Greek theologian, Maximus the Confessor, who had taught that humankind, made in the image of God, was called to grow through prayer and spiritual discipline into the likeness of God. For him, the "likeness" of humankind to God was not to be simply equated with that ineradicable mark of God's making, the *imago Dei,* but was a potentiality, something to be realized through the collaboration with God's grace and the actual practice of living out a Christian life. Nevertheless, a dark shadow falls even on such an optimistic, one might almost say organic, view of humankind, straddling the material and spiritual worlds. For to speak of a growth in likeness also presupposed an unlikeness, an area of dissimilarity, and a tarnishing and occluding of the brightness of the *imago Dei.* But how far is this mere speculation on the part of those early formative Christian thinkers, and is it compatible with the biblical witness?

When we trace the terms "image" and "likeness" back to their biblical roots, we find this pair of words applied to humankind in relation to God in only three passages: Genesis 1:26–27; 5:1 and 9:6. As the Old Testament scholar, Walter Brueggemann (1997, p. 452) insists, these twin terms do not represent a major theological datum for Israel's reflection on humanness. Nevertheless, it is a factor and one that gained prominence through the reflection of the writers of the New Testament as they grappled with the meaning and effect of Christ's appearing. Further, it is significant that all the great figures who appear in the story of the Early Church have written commentaries on the creation stories in the Book of Genesis. And it is in view of this that we return to the Book of Genesis and seek the meaning of the terms of "image" and "likeness." Each of the three passages in which the terms occur belongs to the so-called Priestly school of writing, a literary stratum believed to have been produced during, or soon after, Israel's exile in Babylon (c. 550). The first and key passage reads:

> Then God said, "Let us make humankind in our image, according to our likeness . . ." So God created humankind in his image, in the image of God he created them; male and female he created them (Genesis 1:26–27).

The two words "image" and "likeness" in this passage are not exactly synonymous, but both signify a visual similarity or correspondence between the form of God and humankind. As we have seen, there have been various answers in the history of Christian reflection to the question of where the resemblance might actually lie, and it has been a much debated and contested point. But the roots of the biblical expression lie with the shadow of an object or person that is cast when it is struck by the light of the sun, and not with plastic replicas of the gods, or with ancient notions of divine kingship. As a shadow, the image, in this case, is a shifting and imprecise shape, and so inevitably is a distorted and hazy outline. As such, it precludes any confusion between image and reality. Further, the admittedly infrequent occurrence of the expression "image and likeness" belongs to that strand of Old Testament writing which also records the theophanies, those occasions when something of the mystery of God is communicated to human being, such as when God shows himself to Moses on the holy mount (Exodus 33). Given the origins of the Hebrew expression and its occurrence in this Priestly strand of Hebrew writing with its interest in theophany, one might venture to say the testimony of Genesis 1:26–27 is that the form of humankind, both male and female, has the capacity to reflect, however partially and incompletely, something of the mystery of the divine and to make the divine a visible and tangible reality in the very physicality of human existence. This, of course, is not to say that our human physiognomy is a copy, in the sense of being a model or replica of God, but that the human form has the potential to be a living icon and allow the divine to shine through the very physicality of our being.

The familiar dichotomy drawn in Western thinking, especially since the Enlightenment, between the body and soul, mind and body, is foreign to the symbolic consciousness of the writers of biblical mythology who conceived the human person as being an animated body, if not precisely a psychosomatic being. The second creation myth in Genesis speaks of how the Lord God formed Adam from the moist earth and breathed into his nostrils the breath of life; and so Adam became a living being (Genesis 2:7). A more psychosomatic understanding is presupposed in Paul's writings in the New Testament, where the individual person is evidently constituted as being a physical body, mind and spirit. Thus he writes: "May the God of peace himself sanctify you wholly, and may your spirit and soul and body be kept sound and blameless" (1 Thessalonians 5:23). The view here is that the spirit, mind and physical body constitute an indivisible unity, where the condition of each aspect of a person's being affects the other. This view, as we might say today, is entirely holistic, and presupposes that it is the whole person who falls within the purview of God's creative and redemptive work. Christianity is not simply about the saving of souls, but the making and remaking of the whole person. As Irenaeus insisted, it was the whole embodied person whom God was wanting to save. For it was the whole nature of humankind, both body and soul, which the divine Logos took to himself in the incarnation, and which he had adorned with the graces of the Holy Spirit (see *Against the Heresies* 5.6).

The teaching of Irenaeus entered the very bloodstream of the Eastern tradition of Christianity, and was developed by the seventh-century Greek theologian Maximus the Confessor, whose magnificent theological work defined the relationship between the body and the soul in the human person as a relationship of mutual reciprocity. Although Maximus stated that the human person was a composite being, constituted by a body and soul, he was careful to distinguish between the two terms in order to avoid the implication being drawn that the body and soul formed a kind of synthesis. He said that the soul was embedded in the material reality of the physical body, but the two belonged together, and belonged together so much that the relation of the soul to the body persisted even after the physical death of the person: "we will not," Maximus argued, "accept any abandonment of our bodies."

On the basis of the indissoluble relationship of mutuality between body and soul that Maximus had inherited from the writings of the fourth-century Cappodocian Fathers, Basil of Caesarea, Gregory of Nazianzen and Gregory of Nyssa, Maximus developed the idea that the created human person was a "microcosm of the universe"; for the individual, as soul and body, combined in his or her person the material and intellectual worlds, the physical and spiritual worlds of sense and sensibility. As such the Christian person was called to manifest the unity and reconciliation between the earthly and heavenly realities, which had been achieved through the mystery of Christ's ascension (Ephesians 1:10). For Christ's ascension represented the final festive aspect of the historical salvation wrought by God in Christ, as Maximus wrote in his exposition of the Lord's Prayer:

> after Christ brought his historic work of salvation to completion for our sakes and ascended along with the body he had assumed, he united heaven and earth through himself, connected sensible creation with the intellectual, and so revealed the unity of creation in the very polarity of its elements (cited by von Balthasar, 2003, p. 273).

The Christian body, in other words, becomes the site for the reconciliation of the spiritual and the physical, and itself becomes the medium and instrument through which Christ continues his ongoing work of reconciliation and of uniting all things in himself.

The understanding articulated by Maximus that the human body and soul in some way corresponded and belonged to each other was reaffirmed by the great fourteenth-century Greek theologian and Archbishop of Thessalonica, Gregory Palamas. Palamas was convinced that God's grace worked on the whole embodied person, and not simply with the spiritual faculty of the soul. It was, he argued, the entire person, body and soul together, who was created in the image of God (*Prosopopoeia,* P.G. 150, col. 1361), and so the grace of the Spirit, described as the energies and light of God, could be known and felt in the body as well as in the soul: "In the spiritual person," he wrote, "the grace of the Spirit, transmitted to the body through the soul, grants to the body also the experience of things divine, and allows it the same blessed experiences as the soul undergoes" (*The Triads* 1.ii.12). The implication to be drawn from this is that it is the physical body as well as the soul that can be shaped, enlivened with the divine life, and even irradiated with its heavenly light. Such an experience was precisely what was meant by the term "divinization," understood as an actual participation in the divine life through God's grace (see 2 Peter 1:4, which speaks of Christians being made "partakers of the divine nature"). However, the capacity of the human person to participate in God's life, through grace, was not taken as being part of our innate structure as creatures made in God's image, but was seen as being grounded and made possible by the reality of Christ's incarnation, of God's engagement with the material physicality of human existence in the historic person of Jesus Christ.

There are undeniable inconsistencies and points of tension within the writings of these Greek theologians—Maximus the Confessor and Gregory Palamas—because of the dualistic legacy of Platonic philosophy from which some of their own categories of thought were drawn. The philosopher Plato taught that it was only the soul that could attain the spiritual heights of immortality, which gave rise to the view that the pre-existent and immortal soul was incarcerated in the corporeality of the flesh. But it was the second-century Gnostic teachers, such as Basileides, who viewed material matter as being intrinsically evil. Their message was unequivocal: the flesh is of no avail. This Gnostic view, of course, had been vigorously rebutted by the early Christian apologists, such as the North African, Tertullian, who asserted that the flesh was the very hinge of Christian salvation! Again, in asserting Christian orthodoxy against the claims of Gnosticism, the second-century Bishop of Antioch, Ignatius, as he made his way to an ignominious and horrific martyr's death, insisted that what was seen in the physical pain of Christ's suffering and agonizing death was the very "passion of God" in the flesh. The fact that God had taken human flesh and that Christ had actually suffered and died, was the scandalous and defining particularity of Christianity, setting it apart from the sophisticated systems of Gnostic belief that drove a wedge between God and matter, and the spirit and the flesh.

How, then, are we to read Paul's apparent antithesis between flesh and spirit? The apostle seems to suggest that there is a constant battle between the two. What he was wanting to say, however, rested on a very different premise from either Platonic thought or the nascent ideas of Gnosticism. For Paul, the opposition between flesh and spirit showed itself in patterns of behavior that resulted from misdirected instincts and desires. In addition, where he lists the "works of the flesh" (Galatians 5:19–21a), he draws attention to the kind of behavior that strains and breaks our human and social relationships, and does not denigrate the physical body per se, or particularly focus on those things that we might think of when we hear the expression "sins of the flesh." Indeed, the point drawn through a more attentive reading of this Pauline passage is that our human instincts and drives need to be directed by the Spirit, suggesting that our bodily instincts, what Paul speaks of as the desires of the flesh, can, by God's grace, be directed aright. The logic of what is said is that our passions, far from being suppressed, need to be transformed in order that we might come to express the passion of Christ in the very physicality of our human existence. Christians, we might say, are not to be pale, limp and lifeless, but should be passionate and fully alive.

In concluding this section of our inquiry, we must admit that a somewhat bewildering variety of attitudes towards the body was held in the early centuries of the Christian era, and that the key terms of our exploration, namely "image" and "likeness," are ambiguous and susceptible to different and conflicting interpretations. The tendency towards "inwardness" was accentuated during the time of the Enlightenment with the Cartesian separation of subject and object. But, to some extent, the ensuing opposition of mind and body, matter and spirit, found its checks and balances in the work of artistic creation, in, for example, the portrait paintings of Rembrandt and his pupils, which sought to bring the inward character to light in the very physical features and costume of the individual being painted. The indisputable fact is that human beings are embodied persons and as that most influential of twentieth-century philosophers, Ludwig Wittgenstein, famously remarked, the human body is the best picture of the human soul. It is through and in the body that we relate most immediately both to the natural and to the social worlds, and more recently Paul Ricoeur (1994, p. 54) has written emphatically of "the absolutely irreducible signification of one's own body" in identifying the self and in bringing the "self" to expression.

The terms of our discussion and the ineluctable pull of modernity lead us to conclude that any identification of the *imago Dei* with any particular human quality or faculty is implausible. For whatever it is to speak of the human person created in the *imago Dei*, the *imago Dei* can no longer be located and limited to any interior or relational facet of human life and nature. We have no alternative but to recognize our own bodiliness, and to see the whole person, in his and her corporeal reality, as being the *imago Dei*, which by God's grace can manifest something of the divine in the temporal and spatial conditions of human existence. Quite simply, to assert that a human being is created in the image of God is to speak not only of the inalienable dignity of the human person, but to say that a living human being has the potential, to borrow a phrase from Charles Williams' study of the figure of Beatrice in Dante's *Divine Comedy*, to be a "God-bearing image."

Such a bold assertion returns us to Genesis 1. As we saw, this creation story presents the creation of humankind as the climax and culmination of the divine work of creation. Indeed, in contrast to the making of the sea and sky, land and creatures, all called into being by God's Word, there is a kind of intensity, one might almost say a more direct involvement on God's part in the creation of humankind. What are we to make of this? The prophet to the exiles, in his polemic against idolatry, insists that the God of Israel is incomparable and cannot be visually represented: "To whom then will you liken God, or what likeness compare with him?" (Isaiah 40:18). The question, of course, is rhetorical, but if there can be a possible answer, it seems to point again to the human form. For as the liturgical poet, the prophet's contemporary, lyrically touches on the question as to "who we are," and marveling at the wonder of our making, glimpses a divine aspect of the human form: "what are human beings that you are mindful of them, humankind that you care for them? Yet you have made them a little lower than God, and crowned them with glory and honor" (Psalm 8:4–5).

Here again we are pointed to the mystery of the human person made in the image of and after the likeness of God. But this brings us back to the notion of the *imago* and *likeness*, which we have suggested is necessarily vague in order to safeguard the image becoming, or being seen to be, too concrete, as one might view a model, or a scaled replica. The inherent danger, of which the Hebrew Scriptures are so aware, is that what is taken as an image can easily become an idol, and that, paradoxically, would be the worst distortion. Perhaps one way forward would be to look at another area of discourse and see if there are any particular analogies that might be drawn to move the argument on.

One area that suggests itself is that of aesthetics and the language artists themselves use to describe the artistic project, particularly in the visual arts of drawing, painting and sculpture. In the mid-twentieth century the painter and poet David Jones adopted the suggestive phrase, "hunter of forms," *venator formarum,* to describe the artistic endeavor; but it was the writer and artist Clive Bell who, nearly thirty years previously, coined the expression "significant form" which became a key term in aesthetic theory. Bell (1914, pp. 207–214) claimed that what the stained-glass windows in Chartres Cathedral, Giotto's frescoes at Padua, a Poussin painting, a Persian bowl and a Chinese carpet have in common is "significant form" and that it is precisely this which evokes in the viewer a sense of aesthetic pleasure. Bell cast his net widely, but singled out the work of Paul Cézanne to illustrate that what the artist sought to do through line and color was to show the form of his or her subject. He argued that Cézanne's whole oeuvre captured and expressed the significance of form, and that throughout his career the artist pushed further and further towards a revelation of the significance of form. What Bell says here recalls the frequently quoted view expressed by the artist Paul Klee, that what the artist does is not simply reproduce what he sees, but make it visible. In his *Diaries* Klee records that the very object of artistic making is the shaping of form. The sculptures of Henry Moore and Elizabeth Frink often began as drawings. They would begin by drawing their subjects, and then go on to make other drawings, refining and simplifying the shape with each successive drawing until they were satisfied that what they made revealed the form of their subject. Barbara Hepworth's fascination with form is illustrated by the fact that she frequently used the term in the title she gave to her sculptures.

Perhaps it takes the imaginative eye of the artist to apprehend form and bring it to expression. We might recall how the poet Gerard Manley Hopkins spoke of the "inscape" of a person, an object and its relation to other objects, and how the German poet, and one-time secretary of the sculptor Auguste Rodin, Rainer Maria Rilke, considered the poet's task as giving voice to the "inside" of a thing and allowing it to speak of its own reality.

If the artistic project can be described in these terms of drawing out and revealing of form in the work of art, then we can see it as being analogous to what we mean when we speak of the art of God, of God making and renewing men and women in his image and after his likeness. The art is precisely the drawing out of the image, or form, and therefore it is closely related to the classical concept of *paedea,* or the formation of the person, the drawing out of who a person is and is called to be. Christians, Tertullian said, were made and not born, and our becoming Christian is a process of formation. A crucial factor in this process is time; the forming of the Christian takes time, perhaps even a lifetime: "Like the maturing of fruit on a tree, so the process of Christian formation is long and requires specific conditions" (Clement of Alexandria, *Paedagogus* 2:10) and, as Gregory Palamas insisted, occurs principally when Christians gather together before the mystery of God in worship. The liturgical context of Christian formation will be explored in detail in subsequent chapters, but returning to the "form" as an analogue of "image and likeness" we could recall William Blake's expression, the "human form divine."

This expression, "human form divine," has a poetic quality, and conveniently sidesteps some of the problems that arise when we speak of ourselves as bodies, even bodies made in the image of God. As we have seen, the subject of the body has become a major topic in critical theory and contemporary philosophical reflection and it is commonplace to say that I do not *have* a body, for I *am* a body. The philosopher Friedrich Nietzsche exaggerated the claim when he famously declared: "Body am I entirely" (*Thus Spake Zarathustra,* 1883). This is not to reduce our understanding of the human person to mere anatomy, or to suggest that questions of personal identity are only skin deep. But it does raise an intriguing question: which "body" identifies me? Evidently the body I now have is neither the physical body I had 20 years ago, nor indeed will the body I now have be the exact body I will have in old age. We can, of course, idealize the muscular physical form of the body, as the Renaissance painter and sculptor Michelangelo did, but to speak of the human form affirms our embodied nature without being idealistic or too specific about the body's shape or condition. Indeed, perhaps the recognition of the "human form divine" is not seeing something in ourselves, but, first, a recognition of that form in others:

For Mercy has a human heart,
Pity, a human face;
And Love, the human form divine,
And Peace, the human dress.

William Blake

Following a more theological tack, it could be objected that in swapping the attribution from "image" to "form," the question of where we might locate the *imago Dei* with which we began this inquiry is simply avoided. To meet this objection we could profitably return to Irenaeus, who, as we have seen, carefully drew a distinction between the terms "image" and "likeness." We were made in the image of God and need to grow into the likeness of God. What was intended to be seen in the image, in other words, is more clearly visible in the likeness. For Irenaeus the true likeness into which we are to grow was shown decisively and definitively in Christ. In his scheme of things, until the coming of Christ the "image" was obscure, and the "likeness" was lost to view:

> When, however, the Word of God became flesh, he established two things: for he both truly showed forth the divine image in man, since he became himself what was his image as man, and he established the similitude in a sure manner by assimilating man to the invisible Father (*Against the Heresies* 5.16).

In other words, Jesus Christ is the model pattern and prototype, and at his appearing "the human form divine" is revealed in its full clarity: "by the advent of the Word, the image of God in us appeared in a clearer light." In this sense, the enigma of Genesis 1:26, of humankind being made in the image of God, is finally resolved. Christ is *the* icon of the invisible God (Colossians 1:15), and has made him visible and present in the mundane and mutable theatre of human life and death.

At the beginning of this chapter I attempted to bring art and theology into a kind of dialogue. Art, of course, cannot simply be a substitute for doctrine. We need to articulate Christian understandings in coherently intelligent and convincing ways, but there are points where the truth of what is claimed by Christian doctrine might be brought to light by works of art. The relationship does not work in a single direction however. Indeed, the earliest exponents of Christian faith sometimes drew an analogy between their understanding of God's relationship with humanity and the work of artists. Origen, as we have seen, spoke of the Logos as the painter of the *imago Dei* in humankind, and Athanasius of Alexandria and Augustine of Hippo both drew an analogy between God's work of salvation and the work of the artist. Augustine, in a lyrical passage towards the end of his massive culminating work, *The City of God,* tells of how God, whom he describes as the "Almighty Artist" will refashion the human body, as an artist might recast a disfigured statue and shape a new resurrection body; a body, incidentally, which he believed would be stunningly beautiful! Athanasius, by contrast, suggests that, even in the present time, God begins to get us into shape.

Athanasius regarded the body and soul of an individual person as belonging together; both were seen as being created by God and were the material for his ongoing and purposeful fashioning. Although Athanasius gave precedence to the soul (which he suggested could act as a mirror so that the Christian might contemplate the image of the Father which it reflected), the physical body and the human soul were not opposed to each other, but rather made to complement each other and work together in concert. For as the soul animates the body, so each living body is to bring the soul to expression. And in the end, the decisive factor for each person, what really counted, was whether the individual person actually incarnated and gave bodily expression to the divine love: "For all of us must appear before the judgment seat of Christ, and will receive . . . according to what each one has done in the *body*" (2 Corinthians 5:10).

In his major work, *The Incarnation of the Word of God,* Athanasius revealingly tells the story of God's redemption of humanity in terms of the artist restoring a spoiled portrait. The analogy he draws is presented as a quandary. God's intention was for humankind to become more human, but again and again through history we dehumanize ourselves through acts of violence and self-seeking. So, how was God's purpose to be realized in a world he had created as good, but that was continuously defaced and lacerated by human aggression and our rapacious greed?

What was God to do? What else could he possibly do, being God, but renew his image in humankind. . . . And how could this be done save by the coming of the very Icon of God, our Savior Jesus Christ. . . . You know what happens when a portrait that has been painted on a panel becomes obliterated through external stains. The artist does not throw away the panel, but the subject of the portrait has to come and sit for it again, and then the likeness is redrawn on the same material. (III.14)

The divine artist's material was, of course, the flesh and blood reality of the human person, taken from Mary by the divine Word, in order to portray the true lineaments of the *imago Dei.* This was the art of incarnation, of God becoming flesh in Jesus Christ (John 1:14), and which continued in the actions of the historical Jesus, through his encounters with others, especially in restoring to wholeness those whose lives were crippled with pain and disease. A vivid testimony to this was given by the artist, Vincent Van Gogh (1853–1890). The story of the tortured Dutch artist is well known, as are the iridescent paintings of the later part of his life in Arles; the bright landscapes, cypress trees, and sunflowers, caught in the warm yellow glow of the Mediterranean sun. In his younger days, Van Gogh had felt the call to be an evangelist and took himself off to live and share the drab and impoverished conditions of the peasant workers and miners in the region of the Borinage in Belgium.

Eventually, Van Gogh emerged from the dark and brooding intensity of north European Protestantism into a new climate, where, as we see in his reworking of Rembrandt's etching, *The Raising of Lazarus,* the painting of explicitly religious subjects gave way to a vision of a more sacramental universe fired by the rays of the full sun. The fervent preacher became the fiery painter, applying paint from his palette like a sculptor applying moist clay to a model. But as Van Gogh wrote in a letter to the artist Emile Bernard, at the end of June 1888, it was Christ who had been the supreme artist: "He lived serenely, as a greater artist, despising marble and clay as well as color, working in living flesh . . . this matchless artist made neither statues nor pictures . . . he loudly proclaimed that he made . . . *living* people, immortals." The vision is of Jesus healing the dis-eased and the disfigured, and restoring them to the beauty of the children of God. It would seem that Van Gogh had a good inkling of what it is for humankind to be created in the image of God, and for us to *reflect* something of the brilliance of the divine glory. In any case, this is how he sought to portray men and women, for as he wrote to his brother Theo in the autumn of 1888: "I want to paint men and women with something of the eternal, which the halo used to symbolize, and which we seek to confer by the natural radiance and vibration of our coloring."

The vision of our human bodies transformed by grace and radiant with the reflected splendor of Christ, the true image of the invisible Father, who dwells in unapproachable light, is presented to us in the paintings of that late sixteenth- to early seventeenth-century artist, El Greco (1541–1614). This was in fact the nickname that had been given to Domenicos Theotocopoulos by his friends in Spain, where he finally settled. As an artist, El Greco fused the influences of Christianity, both East and West. He was born in Crete, studied and painted in Venice, then for a shorter time in Rome, and finally settled in the city of Toledo in Spain, a center of fierce Counter–Reformation Catholicism. His earliest works follow the style of the Byzantine icon, but he also learned from the greatest masters of the high Italian Renaissance, including Titian, who, it has been said, invented human flesh in painterly form. We know from an extant inventory of his library that El Greco was a serious reader and student of philosophy. Among his books were a number of key Platonic texts, and some commentators read the elongated figures of his mature paintings as showing a Platonic influence. But the distorted figure is one of the conventional features of the Byzantine style of writing icons. His library contained a number of Eastern liturgical texts, including the Liturgies of St. Basil and St. John Chrysostom, and also works attributed to the Greek writer, Denys (or Dionysius) the Areopagite, including *Celestial Hierarchy,* detailing the orders of angels and offering a cosmic account of the liturgy as the manifestation of the heavenly realities on earth and of the divinization of matter.

As a painter, El Greco developed a unique palette of vibrant primary colors, frequently outlining figures with fine brushstrokes of dazzling white paint. The result in a number of his religious paintings is quite electrifying, portraying human figures incandescent with a divine glory. His landscapes, particularly of the city of Toledo, again show a world as being redolent with grace. This mystical aspect of El Greco's art has sometimes been taken as visual illustration of the mysticism of the sixteenth-century Spanish Carmelites, Teresa of Avila and John of the Cross, but a closer parallel might well be found in the neo-Platonism of the late fifth-century mystical theologian and liturgical commentator, Dionysius the Areopagite. Dionysius presented a vision of a world interpenetrated by the emanation of the divine light and energies of God; the physical world transformed as it is illuminated by the divine light

El Greco, *The Opening of the Fifth Seal (The Vision of St. John)*, 1608–1614 (The Metropolitan Museum of Art, Rogers Fund, 1956 56.48 Photograph, all rights reserved, The Metropolitan Museum of Art)

which descends through the orders of creation and then returns to its source. The correspondence between this religious vision and El Greco's visual language of light and color is so striking that the following lines of Dionysius the Areopagite could well serve as an illuminating caption in an exhibition of his mystical paintings:

> Hierarchy is . . . a sacred order and knowledge and activity which is being assimilated as much as possible to the likeness with God and, in

response to the illuminations that are given it from God, raises itself to the imitation of Him in its own measure (*Celestial Hierarchy* III.1).

A particular painting, which fittingly concludes our exploration of the theme of the image of God, is the so-called *Opening of the Fifth Seal* (see p. 20), originally part of a section for an altarpiece begun in 1608 for the Church of the Hospital at Tavera, a huge project completed by the artist's son, Jorge Manuel. It draws its inspiration from the vision of John on Patmos, as set out in the Book of the Revelation of St. John the Divine. It is a vision of the end time, of the dramatic and final fulfilling of God's purposes. On the left of the canvas is a dressed figure of St. John the Divine, with his arms raised heavenwards, virtually filling the height of the present canvas. In this canvas we see some typical features of El Greco's mature style. There is the play of light reflected by the human forms, as if they themselves were the source of an iridescent light, while the juxtaposition of the colors, blue, yellow, red and green, provides a vibrant background to the composition of the figures. Two groups occupy the center of the canvas, a mixed group of four, two men and two women, and a group of three men, attended by three tumbling cherubic angels. It looks as though the angels have disrobed the figures, which stand naked, and one angel is handing down a white, almost diaphanous, robe to the figure on the right-hand side of the canvas.

In the portrayal of these naked figures, there is no hint of any Platonic spiritualizing away of bodily flesh. The flesh is not relinquished but transformed, as the natural is heightened and drawn into the realm of the spirit. It is sometimes remarked that this is an unfinished painting, with the figures lacking any particular distinguishing features. But this is gratuitous and serves to illustrate our argument that it is not the "perfect body," whether formed by a regimen of diet and exercise, or sculptured by the plastic surgeon, but the human form, a form inclusive of each age and stage of life, gender and racial difference, that is created and remade by God. Returning to the painting, what we see in these painted figures are real *human* forms, and the turning, gestural shapes indicate that they are vivaciously alive. Here are anatomically realistic bodies, but bodies being transformed and destined for glory.

So in El Greco's painterly translation of the vision of John on Patmos we can glimpse something of the human form divine, the form of "human beings," fashioned according to God's image, and called to reflect the very likeness of the incarnate Christ. This is the vision to which the writings of the New Testament bear witness. It is to these foundational documents we must now turn to trace out the model and pattern for our being formed and remade in the likeness of God, and to discover there the vocabulary that articulates this vision of Christianity as a religion of transformation.

2
God's Pattern

In this chapter I intend to focus attention particularly on the writing of the apostle Paul, that most influential architect of Christian thought, but will also look more widely at other documents of the New Testament. Paul employed a whole range of different metaphors to speak of the salvation that was offered and brought by the life, death and resurrection of Christ. A glance at the contents page of books on the theology of Paul will show that most of them deal with such familiar topics as justification, reconciliation, redemption and expiation. But my intention is to follow a less familiar route through his writing and to recover something of his vision of Christianity as a religion of creative transformation. As we will see, this vision is also integral to the testimony of other New Testament writers, as the pivotal place of the story of the transfiguration in the Synoptic Gospels and John's theology of "glory" make abundantly clear. The New Testament bears witness not only to the figure of Jesus Christ as the image of the invisible God, but also to how the Christian might grow into the likeness of Christ by being conformed to the pattern of Christ's death and resurrection. This, as we shall see, is the particular trajectory that we can follow through the writings of the apostle Paul.

Paul's account of God's plan and purpose for humanity centers upon the person of Jesus Christ. For it was the crucified and risen Christ who had confronted Paul on the road to Damascus, and who, according to the tantalizingly brief autobiographical sketch in his letter to the Christian community in Galatia (Galatians 1:13–24) dramatically stopped him in his tracks. The repeated accounts of this encounter on the Damascus road in the Acts of the Apostles suggest that the persecutor of the Church was virtually cornered and confronted by the blinding reality of the One, who, having suffered a cruel death, had been gloriously vindicated by God. The glorious raising-up power of God was dynamite, and, for Paul, any truthful apprehension of the reality of God had from that point on to reckon with the reality of Christ. From now on, it seemed, the only possible way of figuring the divine-human relationship was Christ-shaped. The word used by Paul to describe the content of his experience on the Damascus road was "revelation" "he who had set me apart was pleased to reveal his Son to me" (Galatians 1:13). It was not a question of what was revealed, but who; for this revelation was none other than the appearing of the pre-existent Son of the Father, through whom God had appeared and engaged with his creation.

The language that Paul uses to catch and convey the working out of God's purposes for us, what we mean by the word "salvation," employs the vocabulary of transformation. God's intention is to refashion his creature, and through the operation of the Spirit to renew humanity according to the model of Christ, the eternal Son of the Father: "For those whom he foreknew he also predestined to be conformed to the image of his Son, in order that he might be the firstborn among many brethren" (Romans 8:29). Salvation for Paul is nothing less than our refashioning according to the pattern of Christ, and this understanding has its basis in the conviction that in Christ God had entered into the most radical solidarity with humanity and had identified himself with the whole gamut of human experience. This, as I show, Paul spells out in two key foundational texts:

> "For our sake he made him to be sin who knew no sin, so that in him we might become the righteousness of God" (2 Corinthians 5:21).

and

> "For God has done what the law, weakened by the flesh, could not do: sending his own Son in the likeness of sinful flesh" (Romans 8:3).

When Paul asserts that God "made him to be sin," is he talking exclusively about Christ's ignominious fate of "hanging upon the tree of the cross," or is something also being claimed about Christ sharing the human condition? When the 2 Corinthians 5:21 passage is set alongside the second foundation text, Romans 8:3, we can see that the focus is upon the person of Christ. For God has wrought his saving work in Christ by "sending his own Son in the likeness of sinful flesh." The language of this verse is dense and needs some careful unpacking. The first point to register is that what is spoken of is a divine initiative and action, namely, the "sending of the Son," which, incidentally, is a major and repeated theme in John's Gospel, (see John 3:17; 6:57; 7:29; 11:42; 13:20; 17:18). The sending of the Son was the act of the Father, the impulse of that love which by its very nature seeks to be at one with the object of its love. And as the term "Son" indicates, this is more than an act of communication; in fact, it is a personal engagement of God mediated by the embodied subject, that is, Christ Jesus.

There is, however, an ambiguity in the expression "in the likeness of sinful flesh," but when it is read alongside that stronger statement of Paul's about "Christ being made sin," we can see that something very profound is being said about God's involvement and identification with us and the human predicament. Christ, we might say, was no spectator watching on the sidelines of all the mess and marvel of human living, but was there in the very thick of it. The sending of the Son in the likeness of sinful flesh, therefore, must entail a full sharing in the conditions of human existence, a sharing of our embodied and fleshly existence: "when the time had fully come, God sent forth his Son, born of a woman" (Galatians 4:4). The logic of what Paul writes compels us to use the language of incarnation, to speak of God becoming *enfleshed.* John's Gospel speaks of the Word being made flesh, and the point to register in this expression is that the change is predicated of God himself: the Word *became* flesh (John 1:14), became incarnate, as a disciple of Paul might say, in order that God might be fully embodied in Christ (see Colossians 1:15–19).

This sense of fullness is actually detected further in Romans 8, where Paul intimates that the "sending of the Son" is nothing less than a total and utterly generous giving over of the divine life into the vicissitudes of human life in the world. For it is the very condition of human nature, with all its contradictions, appetites, needs and aspirations, which the incarnate Christ shared, suffered and struggled with. Such a conviction accords with Paul's insistence that God's great work of salvation is perfected in "our human weakness" (2 Corinthians 12:9; cf. 1 Corinthians 1:25). This Pauline expression resonates with the vocabulary of solidarity that we find used by the writer of the Epistle to the Hebrews, such as the passage speaking of Christ being "made like his brothers and sisters in every way" (Hebrews 2:17); and similarly, "For we do not have a high priest who is unable to sympathize with our weaknesses, but one who in every respect has been tempted as we are" (Hebrews 4:15).

However, in stressing Christ's radical identification with humanity in the incarnation, we must be careful not to suggest that it was an evacuation of divinity, or the total playing out of the divine life through his humiliation and death. For to construe the incarnation in such a way would be to foreshorten the "sending," and prematurely halt that passage of divine salvation, which is finally both a reaching out and a return. The Son is sent and, as repeatedly stated in John's Gospel, returns to the Father. This parabola pattern of reaching out in compassionate solidarity and return can also be traced from that most lyrical and poetic of passages, the so-called "Christ-hymn" in Philippians 2:6–11:

> though Christ was in the form of God, he did not count equality with God a thing to be held on to, but emptied himself, taking the form of a servant, being born in human likeness. And being found in human form he humbled himself and became obedient to death, even to death on a cross. Therefore God has highly exalted him and bestowed on him the name that is above every name . . . Jesus Christ is Lord to the glory of God the Father.

In this passage Paul speaks of the Son both being in the *form* of God and of his taking the *form* of a slave. The term "form" is clearly crucial to the passage and extends the language of "image" and "likeness" beyond the sense of the word "similarity," which in every case, of course, invariably entails an element of dissimilarity. The word "form" is far stronger than the word "shape" and has the ring of a technical term, denoting what a thing is, its essential quality and character, rather than its external features and appearance (see Fee, 1995, p. 204). To paraphrase, we might say that since Christ was truly God, he came to share the reality of our human predicament. Such a reading runs parallel to our foundational text, Romans 8:3, which speaks of Christ "in the likeness of sinful flesh" and evokes that sense of incarnation that we find in the Gospel and First Letter of John. The testimony of John is that the eternal Son of the Father revealed the divine life in human form ("whoever has seen me has seen the Father" [John 14:9b]) through the mutual reciprocity of the divine and human life ("I am in the Father and the Father in me" [John 14:10c]) in one undivided life ("I and the Father are one" [John 10:30]). So far then, we have sought to tease out the meaning of two short texts from Paul's writing; this forms the basis from which Paul can mint a language that speaks of our human transformation in Christ and through the Spirit.

The vocabulary of "form," "image" and "likeness" brings us to the very heart of Paul's writing in the Second Letter to the Corinthians and recalls significant parallels elsewhere in the corpus of the New Testament. The primary route we shall follow is through 2 Corinthians. Now, whether this letter is a conflation of two or more letters of the apostle is immaterial, for the passages that immediately concern us, chapters 3 and 4, cohere and flow as a single argument. We have already alluded to the matters that probably led Paul to write again to the church in Corinth, but to say who his opponents were is little more than intelligent guesswork. Whoever they were, they were evidently undermining Paul's authority as a teacher, and his standing in the church as an apostle. So Paul has to set out his credentials, which he did elsewhere—for example in Philippians—and rehearses again what it means to be an apostle. In 2 Corinthians what Paul says about the life and fate of an apostle shades out and applies to all those who are called and caught up in the apostolic life and mission of the whole people of God. For the letter is addressed to the whole church at Corinth, to all those in the whole region of Achaia, who are called to manifest the Spirit (2 Corinthians 1:1b). So what Paul sets out in this correspondence is not a case of special pleading, or straightforwardly a riposte to his opponents (whoever they were), but applies generally, to all who are called Christian. Indeed, one would say that what is said in the passages which we shall look at has bearing on what is involved in being, or more precisely becoming, a Christian.

For Paul, as for all Christians down the centuries, the beginning of Christian life is to be found in the waters of baptism. The Greek verb "to baptize" used in the New Testament refers to a dramatic action; what comes to mind is not a gentle sprinkling of water, but a real saturation, a real soaking. So talk of baptism demands dramatic imagery! Baptism, we might say, is like the meeting of two rivers, the flow of human faith and love into an unending stream of divine life, making the place of baptism a whirlpool of water; a place of swirling waters, whose current draws down those who would enter into it, down even into the deep waters of death. It is not that through baptism the Christian merely imitates the fate of Jesus, but that in being baptized the reality of Christ's death is brought to bear and impresses itself upon the one being baptized. Thus in speaking of those who entered the waters of baptism, Paul can say, with full rhetorical force: "Do you not know that all of us who were baptized into Christ Jesus were baptized into his death? We were buried therefore with him by baptism into death" (Romans 6:3 and 4a). In this passage we can pick up that critical preposition "with" and, as in a game of snap, link the baptism of Jesus with that of the Christian to say that as God in Christ came to be identified *with* humanity on the banks of the river Jordan, so through the water of baptism the Christian becomes identified *with* Christ. For Paul the terminology is crucial, since this dying "with Christ" enables the believer literally to become incorporated, that is, to be "in Christ." The expression is more than a turn of phrase and occurs at crucial junctures in the writing of Paul where he spells out the very basis of Christian existence, life and hope (see Romans 16:7; 1 Corinthians 15:22; 2 Corinthians 5:17 and 21). The expression "in Christ" is close to a technical term and signals a real share and participation of the Christian in the life of Christ. So, to speak of the Christian being "in Christ" is to speak of an actual participation, a real sharing on the part of the Christian in the very life and being of the crucified and risen Christ. By entering into the deep waters of Baptism, the Christian "dies with Christ," and as one commentator neatly summarizes the matter, "dying *with* Christ is the way to become *in* Christ" (Ziesler, 1988, p. 93). Our being "in Christ" is the very sharing of Christ's life, which continually shapes and refashions the person until they come to resemble more clearly the likeness of Christ himself.

For Paul, then, baptism is the definitive and objective means whereby the Christian is *conformed* to Christ, the dramatic beginning of an ongoing process whereby the Christian is shaped according to the pattern of Christ's passion, suffering and resurrection. We know little about the actual ritual practice of Christian baptism at the time of Paul, but the language he uses in Romans 6, of the Christian being "buried *with* Christ" would suggest a literal going down into the water, as Christ died and was buried. Other passages suggest that the candidate was stripped and then clothed during the act of baptism, a ritual action which gave rise to the expressions of "putting on Christ," but the primary metaphor is undoubtedly that of "dying with Christ," and this was understood to be effectively and definitively enacted in the ritual action of baptism. In this chapter of Romans, Paul speaks of the "old nature" being "crucified with him," and in a more autobiographical passage elsewhere, Paul speaks of sharing in Christ's sufferings and more pointedly, being shaped by the form of his death (Philippians 3:10). What could this possibly mean? The point, of course, is that this "sharing of Christ's sufferings" is precisely a sharing of Christ's sufferings, and is not to be confused with the pain or misfortune that the individual Christian might at any time feel or suffer. For some, sharing Christ's suffering might involve being alongside those who suffer, but in every case, it entails that self-surrender that we see in the Christ of Gethsemane, the willing handing over of oneself to be shaped by the circumstances and events of one's life.

In 2 Corinthians 4:10–11, Paul speaks of being "given up to death." The expression echoes the language of the Passion narrative in the Synoptic Gospels, thereby indicating that the suffering of the apostle was directly related to the passion of Christ himself. So this reference extends and deepens the meaning of what it was to be an apostle. The apostle was not only to proclaim the gospel, but actually to exhibit it, to represent it, as it were, in his own person. For what is being said here is that the apostle actually *embodied* the crucified and risen Christ through his own suffering: "we are always given up to death for Jesus' sake, so that the life of Jesus may be manifested in our mortal flesh" (2 Corinthians 4:11). What is spoken of here is more than a matter of imitation, or the apostle modeling himself on Christ; for the logic of Paul's argument leads to the conclusion that it was precisely through the apostle's suffering that Christ was formed and embodied in those to whom they had been sent. Furthermore, it was also through this Christ-like passion that the apostles drew out the form of Christ in those to whom they preached and bore apostolic witness: "So death is at work in us, but life in you" (2 Corinthians 4:12). This same sense is intensified in Galatians, where Paul uses the startling metaphor of the birth pangs of a mother bringing new life into the world to describe the sufferings of the apostle: "My little children, with whom I am again in travail until Christ be formed in you" (Galatians 4:19).

Paradoxically, then, the pattern of Christ's passion and self-giving gives way to life and an irrepressible hope, and the often unexpected emergence and expression of hope in the life of a Christian is the outcome of the power of God to raise us up. Christian hope is a sign of resurrection. It is the gift of the one who in his dying descended into the darkest caverns of death and in whose glorious resurrection reached out, as is so graphically depicted in the Easter icon of the Christian East known as the *Anastasis,* to grasp the hand of humanity and draw us into the brightness of God's transforming presence. Paul testifies that Christ was raised by the glory of the Father (Romans 6:4) while the Gospel of John designates the crucifixion as the very hour of Christ's glorification. This reference to "glory" and the Johannine paradox of glorification brings us to the edge of language and to the place of vision and wonder. Like every paradoxical statement, the paradoxical language of cross and glory points beyond itself and depicts a human body (that of the incarnate Jesus) who, being disfigured by suffering and death, was fully transformed and shot through with the radiant brilliance of the undying divine life and love. The Hebrew prophet had announced God's intention of "doing a new thing" (Isaiah 42:9; 43:19; 48:6), and for Paul the Easter happening was that new event; that new event against which all comparisons proved inadequate. It was as though all categories failed to capture or convey the reality of Christ, the crucified and risen Lord. Indeed, Paul was so convinced and compelled by this "new" thing in the resurrection of Jesus that he had no option but to jettison his previous ways of thinking and reckoning, for as he admits: "even though we once regarded Christ from a human point of view, we regard him thus no longer" (2 Corinthians 5:16). The implication of what Paul is saying here is that whatever picture one might construct of the historical Jesus it is, at best, misleading, for it is the death and resurrection (death and resurrection *together*) that manifests the hidden *form* of Christ.

The point Paul is making in 2 Corinthians 5:16 is not simply that Christ eludes description, but that the reality of Christ can only be apprehended and made visible when the Christian is *conformed* to the crucified and risen Christ, who is the new creation and firstborn of the dead. The form of Christ, revealed in his death and resurrection together, in other words, provides the template according to which the life of the baptized is to be shaped: "when you were buried with [Christ] in baptism, you were also raised with him" (Colossians 2:12). What it means for the Christian to be conformed to Christ is for that person to be shaped into the same form as Christ. As we have already seen, Paul's account of the pattern of apostolic life, like his references to the Christian's "dying with Christ," invariably leads to a reference to the resurrection, of that work of God in making new. Paul says, in a key passage we must return to later, that he presses on "to know Christ and the power of his resurrection and may share his sufferings, becoming like him in his death, that if possible I may attain the resurrection from the dead." The very pattern of suffering and resurrection, we might say, so impresses itself upon Paul that his life is continuously being reshaped so that it may reveal and manifest the form of Christ himself.

The vocabulary and the sequence of Paul's thought not only traces a trajectory through suffering, death and resurrection, but presupposes a correspondence between the fate of Christ and that of the making of a Christian. This correspondence is demonstrated in the very structure of Paul's letter to the Christian community at Philippi, with chapter 3 being a mirror image of chapter 2. In chapter 3 Paul enunciates how the Christian may make Christ visible, and in chapter 2 he celebrates how the invisible God took visible shape in the person of the incarnate Christ. The correspondences implied by a shared vocabulary speak of a dynamic exchange and posit a relationship of dependence between the shape of Christian life and hope and the person and fate of Christ Jesus. The point is most clearly demonstrated when set out in diagrammatic form as in Figure 1.

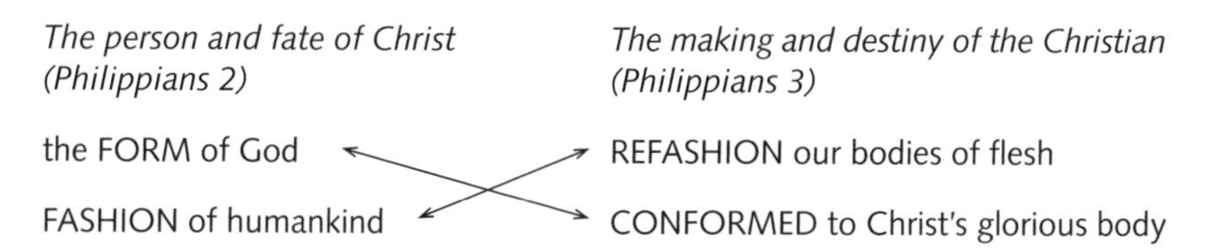

Figure 1 The formational exchange of divine and human life

In these two chapters Paul artfully and most clearly speaks of the fate of Christ as opening a pathway for a human participation in the divine life. By assuming human flesh, and through his suffering and death, Christ opens the path to glory through being exalted by God. Similarly, in the Letter to the Hebrews, Christ is described as being "the pioneer and perfecter of our faith" (Hebrews 12:2). In this letter, as in the Pauline corpus, we find an emphasis being placed upon the suffering and glorification of Christ as the pattern that each Christian must replicate in his or her actions, attitudes and bodily disposition. The entering into and sharing of Christ's suffering is inextricably bound up with glorification and resurrection. But when might the Christian come to know the power of resurrection? The writings of Paul preclude any single or exclusive answer to this question.

The hope of resurrection undoubtedly orientates and opens the Christian towards God's future. For it is at the *parousia,* at the end of time, when the dead will be raised, and so the resurrection is clearly a future goal. This eschatological understanding finds its clearest expression in 1 Corinthians 15:44 ff., which speaks of the definitive fulfillment of God's purposes. The final transformation, in other words, will be at the *parousia,* when "all shall be changed" (1 Corinthians 15:51). This sense of resurrection as both promise and future prospect, occurring at the end of time, is also explicit in Paul's letter to the Philippians, where he writes: "we await a Savior, the Lord Jesus Christ . . . who will change our humble body so that it is conformed to his glorious body, by the working of him who is able to subject all things to himself" (Philippians 3:21). The dawn of the *parousia,* the turn of the ages, it seems, will be marked by the in rush of glory, and the whole created order will be shot through with the transforming presence of the divine life. In the end, God will be "all in all" (1 Corinthians 15:28).

However, alongside the understanding of the individual Christian's hope of a future resurrection from the dead, Paul suggests that the power of the resurrection is also operative in their present embodied lives. It is as though the full weight of God's future presses down, or rather impresses itself upon, the present time and experience of the Christian. Thus, just a few verses earlier in this Philippians' passage, Paul confidently speaks of coming to know the power of Christ's resurrection before he mentions the goal of a "resurrection out of, and from, the dead." Being "in Christ," says Paul, means "to know him and the power of Christ's resurrection *(anastaseos),* and sharing Christ's sufferings, so as to be conformed to his death, and to attain the resurrection *(ex-anastasin)* from the dead" (Philippians 3:10, my translation). I have included the transliterated Greek vocabulary of the term "resurrection" in brackets to illustrate a possible distinction between a present experience of the power of resurrection, and the resurrection from the dead as future goal.

Such a distinction between present experience and future hope could also be adduced from the sequence of thought expressed in this compact sentence. Here Paul speaks of knowing Christ in (1), the power of Christ's resurrection and (2), participation in Christ's suffering, in order that he might (3), attain to the resurrection of the dead. Set out in this way, we can see how Paul's language and logic point in the same direction, and the implication of what he is saying is clearly evident. A direct allusion to the present experience of resurrection is made in Ephesians 2:5 and 6: "even when we were dead through our trespasses, [God] made us alive together with Christ . . . and raised us up with him." Whether these words were penned by Paul or by a disciple of his, it would be reasonable to conclude that although the emphasis in Paul's writings undoubtedly falls on the Christian's fate of sharing Christ's suffering (as J. Dunn rightly insists (1998, p. 487)), the Christian can also (though this is excluded by Dunn) come to know what I have described above as the "raising-up power of God" as a present experience in the vicissitudes of their lived lives.

Not surprisingly, then, the sense of the power of Christ's resurrection being manifest in the present embodied existence of the Christian is expressed by Paul in a passage in which he enunciates that it is through the apostle's suffering that the life of Jesus shows itself:

> always carrying in the body the death of Jesus, so that the life of Jesus may also be made visible in our bodies. For while we live, we are always being given up to death for Jesus' sake, so that the life of Jesus may be made visible in our mortal bodies (2 Corinthians 4:10–11).

In John's Gospel the question of how the Christian participates in the death and resurrection of Jesus is refigured in the so-called Bread of Life discourse, following the sign of the miraculous feeding of the multitude. Unlike the manna given to the Israelites in the wilderness, the bread that Jesus gives is his flesh given for the life of the world. This bread depicts his passion and death and the deliberate symbolism would have resonated with the Eucharist faith and practice of the evangelist's community. In John 6 we can detect a similar dialectic between time present and a future promise; for instance, "he who eats my flesh and drinks my blood *has eternal life,* and *I will* raise him up at the last day" (John 6:54). So in its sacramental mode, the Christian's participation in the Eucharist is seen by John as the means by which the individual Christian can come to share in and appropriate Christ's death and resurrection. Significantly, this discourse reaches its conclusion with a reference to the spirit, and the ringing assertion that "It is the spirit that gives life" (John 6:63).

Paul understands Christ to have been raised from the dead through the Spirit, and argues that it is the same Spirit that is even now given to the Christian as a guarantee (arrabon, 2 Corinthians 1:22; 5:5, literally meaning a down payment of what will be fully given; and compare, Ephesians 1:13–14) of their future hope. This Greek word, *arrabon,* carries the sense of something being anticipated, suggesting therefore that even now our mortal bodies might feel a twinge of the resurrection body and assume a tinge of reflected resurrection glory. To draw an analogy, one might say that the resurrection runs as a trailer in time of that ultimate film of God's final purposes. The gift of the Spirit to the Christian is God's eschatological gift, and the freight it carries is nothing less than glory and life. Furthermore, the very presence of the Spirit is experienced as gift, and is operative in the renewal of the person who is "in Christ."

So one could say that the reality of the resurrection is reflected back into present time and manifests itself in ways that can only be alluded to, as noted above, by speaking of "newness" and of the person in Christ being "made new" in the here and now. The range and application of this language of "newness" are clearly illustrated in the following concatenation of Pauline texts:

> Though our outer humanity is wasting away, our inner humanity is being made *new* day by day (2 Corinthians 4:16; compare Colossians 3:10)

> If anyone is in Christ, he is a new creation, the old has passed away, behold, the *new* has come (2 Corinthians 5:17).

> For neither circumcision, nor uncircumcision counts for anything, but a *new* creation (Galatians 6:15).

And further, those who are "in Christ," are called and empowered by the indwelling Spirit, to make visible the character of what John Taylor has called "the Christ-like God," thereby, making transparent the source of their new life in their way of life and ways of relating to others:

> present your bodies as a living sacrifice. . . . Do not be conformed to this world but be transformed by the renewal of your mind, that you may prove what is acceptable to God (Romans 12:2).

> Be renewed in the spirit of your minds, and put on the new humanity, created after the likeness of God in true righteousness and holiness (Ephesians 4:23–24).

What can be said, then, is that the resurrection is both a future hope and a present process of renewal, even of being newly made. To draw a musical analogy, we could say that for Paul the theme of resurrection is double tracked; it is the distant but certain triumph song of the risen Christ, but its rhythm is also felt in the very beating pulse of the living Christian in communion with Christ.

In the present, "to know the power of the resurrection" is to embody in one's own person, and to bring to expression through one's thoughts, words and actions, the crucified and risen Christ, who is none other than "the likeness of God" (2 Corinthians 4:4) and the icon or "image of the invisible God" (Colossians 1:15). As a disciple of Paul might say, the individual believer is constantly being reshaped, made new, in order that they might come to reveal more fully the form of Christ. That form is none other than the inclusive form of a new humanity, transcending differences of race and gender, and constantly being renewed "after the image of its creator" (Colossians 3:10). The echo here of the creation of humankind in Genesis 1:27, serves to underline that what it means for the Christian to show more fully the form of Christ is for the person to become more human, not less, and for their humanity to be enlarged and enhanced, to the measure of that mature humanity shown in Christ Jesus (Ephesians 3:13; cf. Colossians 1:28).

To recap the argument so far, we can say that the death and resurrection of Christ reveal the *form* of Christ, and that what is entailed in the Christian being conformed to the image of God's Son (Romans 8:29) is for that person to be shaped by the *pattern* of Christ's death and resurrection. This process of being conformed to Christ is undoubtedly part of a lifelong process, and, as such, is part of a wider process of transformation. Indeed, when a person is perfectly conformed to Christ, then that person is *transformed* in Christ, or to use the poet Edwin Muir's striking phrase: "And so transmuted stand[s] beyond all change."

The reference to transformation brings us to the final term in Paul's account of what it is for a person to become what God calls them to be. Paul's usage of the verb "to transform" and its cognates has a particular vibrancy and spells out most fully what is entailed in the formation of Christians, which is nothing less than a total remaking and refiguring of the whole person. In thus pointing to the goal of Christian formation the term "transformation" brings into focus a frequently overlooked dimension of Christian existence, namely, the visual and contemplative dimensions of Christian life and prayer. The people of God are invited "to look to the Lord and to be radiant" (Psalm 34:5; see also Isaiah 60:1–6), and to behold the transforming glory of God, for which, according to both Paul and John, they are destined. Again, the promised "glorification" is not solely a future hope to which the Christian looks forward, but is taken as being operative even in the present time. In the so-called "high priestly prayer" in John's Gospel, Jesus addresses the Father and declares: "the glory which you have given me I have given them" (John 17:22). In Romans 8:30, Paul confidently declares that those whom God has "called he also justified; and those whom he justified he also glorified." The grammar of these two statements indicates an accomplished, but ongoing process; the divine glory is given or, more precisely, shown, and being so manifest is able to be reflected back as the recipient is gradually transformed with increasing splendor. For what is shown is nothing less than the sheer brilliance of the divine presence, whose light can transform and transfigure those upon whom it shines with its celestial brightness. It is significant that having asserted that Christians are already glorified, Paul continues in this chapter of Romans to enumerate a number of difficulties and kinds of suffering. The flow of the argument therefore suggests that however disfiguring our human distress, dislocation and suffering might be, it cannot totally erase the reflected glory, which is received by those who are faced with God's gracious countenance in Christ Jesus (Romans 8:35–37; see also 2 Corinthians 6:4–5). Indeed, as Paul insists, there are no conceivable circumstances, either in life or in death, in which the Christian might be hidden from the loving and transforming gaze of Christ.

At the end of chapter 3 of 2 Corinthians, Paul spells out the process of transformation in terms of contemplation, and explains how the Christian comes to reflect the divine glory manifested in the face of Jesus Christ (2 Corinthians 4:6), by drawing upon the Hebrew Scriptures that tell of how Moses communed with God on Mount Sinai. The overall passage is part of Paul's apologia, which, he argues, was validated by the manifestation of Christ through the Spirit in the very lives of the Christian community in Corinth. More immediately in this chapter, Paul draws a contrast between the Jewish and Christian dispensations: the Covenant of the Law, which became fixed in hardened patterns of behavior, and the New Covenant being presently realized by the enlivening Spirit of the living God in Christ (see Romans 8:11). The prophets Jeremiah and Ezekiel had declared the promise of a new covenant in which human hearts would be remolded closer to God's desire through the future gift of the Spirit (Jeremiah 31:31–34; Ezekiel 36:26). For Paul the time of fulfillment had come, and the evidence was visible in the life of the Christian community: "you show yourselves as being a letter of Christ delivered by us, inscribed not with ink, but with the Spirit of the living God, not on tablets of stone, but on your hearts of flesh" (2 Corinthians 3:3).

With the fulfilling of the promise through the momentous victory of Christ and the release of the Spirit, the time had come for the Law to be set aside. It was to be regarded as being obsolescent and as transient as the glory that accompanied the giving of the Law to Moses on Mount Sinai. In presenting this case, Paul uses a conventional method of rabbinic argument from Scripture, technically known as a Midrash. But whatever the precise method he employed, in the end, Paul transmits his own message and follows his own logic to demonstrate the working out of God's final transformative project.

What Paul does in this passage at the end of chapter 3 is to draw from a number of scriptural texts in order to weave the rich textured language of transformation. The Jewish Rabbis were, of course, adept at reading across two or more texts in order to produce a new reading or understanding and form of verbal expression. Paul too, it seemed, was skilled in this rabbinic method of interpreting Scripture and producing a new meaning, or Midrash. His pen, we might say, dripped with the Hebrew Scriptures, and without unraveling all the scriptural resonances of this passage in 2 Corinthians 3, we might trace some of the prominent strands back to the Book of Exodus, chapters 33 and 34:29 f., and possibly to Numbers 12:1–8 as well. The passage from the Book of Numbers is an oracle that condenses the Sinai narratives in the Book of Exodus. In this oracle, the Lord tells Aaron and Miriam that unlike the other prophets, he spoke with Moses "face to face," and, more strikingly, promises that Moses would see the very "form of the Lord." Of the two

Exodus passages in view, one tells of how Moses ascended the holy Mount of Sinai to receive the Law, and the other tells of how Moses' face became radiant with the divine glory as he communed with God "face to face." Paul's use of these Scriptures is not straightforward, and his reference to two veils can easily confuse the reader. But what is clear is the recorded fact that when Moses turned and left the mountain to return to the people of Israel, the reflected glory in his face faded, and he veiled his face. It was as if the Israelites could not bear to see what Moses had been privileged to see, namely, the very "glory of the Lord." Paul follows this line of the narrative in Exodus 34:29 f. and then, as we have seen, introduces a reference to a veil obscuring the perception of his Jewish contemporaries. The second reference serves as a metaphor for their failure to recognize that God's glory is uniquely revealed in the incarnate, crucified and risen Christ. So he argues that when Jews read the Torah, a veil covers their face, its meaning is obscured. On the other hand, in the new dispensation a true understanding is possible, with the appearing of the gospel of the glory of Christ (2 Corinthians 4:4).

The logic of Paul's argument leads us to conclude that when believers "turn to the Lord" they receive a glory that, far from fading, increases in intensity until it brings them to the *parousia,* to that final state of glorification when they behold God "face to face." Paul's use here of the present tense of the verb "to transform" indicates that the process of this change or transformation operates in the present time when the Christian "turns to the Lord," that is, when he or she directs his or her contemplative attention upon Christ. What the Christian perceives in the face of Jesus Christ, is none other than the glory of the creator God himself (see 2 Corinthians 4:6), and through contemplating the face of Christ the Christian comes to reflect that same glory, "from one degree of glory to another" (2 Corinthians 3:18). The grammar of this verse is complex: it indicates that God himself is the source of "glory," and also suggests that the process of transformation is progressive, that Christians are transformed by one degree of glory after another. We are changed, we might say, into that which we contemplate. As the most eloquent orator of the ancient Eastern Church, John Chrysostom, put it: "Not only do we behold the glory of God, but from it receive also a sort of splendor" (*Homilies* VII).

But how, the reader might ask, does such a conviction sit alongside the point registered in Paul's earlier correspondence with the Corinthians, where he argues that at the present time the Christian "sees but in a glass dimly, but then, face to face" (1 Corinthians 13:12)? The theme of eschatological fulfillment is a constant and consistent one in Paul's writings, but when he speaks in this passage of our seeing "in a mirror dimly," he is saying that our human perception of God is, at best, a hazy outline. The same point might well be adduced from his assertion that "we walk by faith, and not by sight" (2 Corinthians 5:7). The point at issue is our human perception, of what we as human beings are able to apprehend, and therefore what Paul writes here parallels what he says elsewhere about our knowledge of God, namely, that what counts is not *our* claim, or capacity to know God, but God knowing us (see 1 Corinthians 13:12b).

Similarly, the perspective in 2 Corinthians 3 is of God facing the believer in the person of Christ, so that our "turning to the Lord" is a response to the shining of the divine countenance in the face of Christ and the enlightenment of the gospel. The dynamic at work here in this contemplative attitude is the Spirit. It is the Spirit that opens the doors of perception and frees the believing "self" to be what the Christian is called to become. Unsurprisingly, then, these passages where Paul speaks of glorification refer to and invoke the role of the Spirit. The clear implication to be drawn is that it is the Spirit that effects the "transforming" work of God in those who "turn to the Lord." Thus, to return to our passage, we might paraphrase 2 Corinthians 3:18 in these terms: "We all, with unveiled face, presently contemplating the glory of Christ, are being changed into his likeness, from one degree of glory to another, which is of the Lord's making, through the Spirit."

Such a reading of Paul's writings is reminiscent of what became known by the theologians of the Early Church as *theosis,* or the divinization of the Christian person, a doctrine that came to prominence in the theology of Eastern Christianity. This doctrine trades on the exchange between the divine and human life through the incarnation. It was first enunciated by Irenaeus, but again, has deep roots in Paul's conviction that although Christ was rich, yet for our sake he became poor, so that by his poverty we might become rich (2 Corinthians 8:9). At its most explicit, the doctrine teaches that as the divine Logos, or Word, has taken to himself the stuff of humanity in its flesh and blood reality, so those who are "in Christ" are called to become "partakers of the divine nature" (2 Peter 1:4), an expression, of course, which draws the Pauline language of participation to its final logical conclusion. In elucidating this doctrine, the Fathers of the Early Church came to give priority to the Spirit as the operating agent in this process of exchange. Cyril, the formidable fifth-century Patriarch of Alexandria, for example, made the central role of the Spirit explicit when he said: "Participation in the Holy Spirit gives human beings the grace to be shaped as a complete copy of the divine nature." Such participation in the divine nature was seen as the perfect communion of the embodied person with the Triune God. For anyone, he says, who receives the image of the Son, that is the Spirit, possesses thereby in all fullness the Son, and the Father who is in him" (cited by Clement, 1993, p. 264).

The formula of the fourth ecumenical Council of Chalcedon (451) set limits on speculation as to how the divine and human could coexist in the one person, and insisted that the human and divine natures of Christ were a perfect conjunction, without confusion or separation. In the New Testament, John's Gospel testifies that it was in the humanity of the Incarnate Word that "we beheld his glory" (John 1:14b), whereas in the Synoptic tradition, the glory of Jesus is revealed in one extraordinary incident, the transfiguration of Jesus on the mount. The incident is deliberately placed by the evangelists at that point in their narrative where Jesus resolutely makes his way towards Jerusalem, the place where he would meet hostility, suffering and death. In this way, the story reveals the divine intention to transform those human faces disfigured and distorted by pain and anguish.

At this point, then, we see a thematic correspondence with the Pauline passage in 2 Corinthians 3. The most obvious linkage is seen in the use of the term "transformation" in Mark and Matthew's accounts of how Jesus was transfigured on the Mount (Matthew 17:1–8; Mark 9:2–8). In this narrative the verb *metamorpho* does not mean a literal change in form, but the making visible of the likeness of divine glory in human form, in the person of Christ Jesus. However we interpret the event of the transfiguration, the narrative is evidently a visionary story. For on the mount the disciples Peter, James and John saw Jesus radiant with the luminous splendor of the God who dwells in "unapproachable light." Jesus' physical body radiated the sheer brilliance of the divine life: "his face shone like the sun, and his garments became white as light" (Matthew 17:2; see also 2 Peter 1:16–18). This aspect is accentuated by Luke, who describes the experience of the disciples as a visionary experience of the divine glory, the dazzling radiant beauty of God that has dawned upon our darkened world with Christ's appearing (cf. the songs of the birth and infancy narratives in Luke 1:78–79; 2:14 and 32). As they looked at the figure of Jesus on the mount, what met the eyes of the disciples was our very "human likeness" shot through with the life of God. No wonder, then, that they were overwhelmed, literally awestruck as they recognized Jesus as the Christ of glory, resolutely set, as Isaiah's Suffering Servant, to enter the darkness of anguish, suffering, and death. But the vision shows even more, for the transfiguration was also an epiphany, and as such is reminiscent of the story of Jesus' baptism. For then, as on the mount, there is a reference to the divine voice confirming the mysterious identity of Jesus as the Son of God. The responses of the three disciples privileged to witness the event suggest that the incident was but a momentary glimpse of Christ's divine nature that was finally revealed through the mystery of his death and resurrection. In terms of the liturgical poetry of the Byzantine tradition, what was revealed to the disciples on Mount Tabor (the traditional setting of the transfiguration) was nothing less than the luminous beauty of the Form of God in the human body of the incarnate Jesus Christ.

The reference in Mark and Matthew to the timing of the transfiguration, "after six days" (Mark 9:2, Matthew 17:1), is not an incidental detail but a deliberate symbolic allusion to the six days of creation enumerated in Genesis 1, suggesting that what was revealed on the holy mount was a privileged preview of God's recreation at the end of time, of God's ultimate intention to "create a new heaven and a new earth" (Revelation 21:1; cf. 2 Peter 3:13). The symbolism of God's new creation is even more explicit in the reference to "the eighth day" in Luke's narrative of the transfiguration (Luke 9:28–36). The numbering is not simply a neat rounding up of the days of the week, but specifies the eighth day, the day of resurrection and new creation. In the transfiguration, in other words, we also glimpse a preview of the final form of human nature redolent with and reflecting the glory of divine grace. This premonition of the new creation on the mount of transfiguration shows how our human flesh and blood reality can become the stuff from which glory is made. Perhaps the final word in our survey could be that of the elder John, who in his first letter assured the community to which he wrote that although in the present time we might not know exactly what we shall be, we know that when Christ appears, we shall be as he is (1 John 3:2).

In this chapter I have traced Paul's understanding of the basis and process of Christian salvation and in doing so have shown how the vocabulary he uses to articulate this divine work provides us with a rich word-field, which encompasses the key terms in our thesis that the actual practice of Christianity is essentially a process of personal transformation—the transformation of the person to reflect more fully the likeness of Christ within a community of persons, the community of the baptized, constituting the very Body of Christ. In this process, each person is summoned to become what they are called to be and enabled to become, through the gracious working of the risen Christ and the Holy Spirit. A telling phrase is found in the Letter to the Ephesians that speaks of Christians as being God's "workmanship, created in Christ Jesus," and the vocabulary used in this text suggests that the remaking of the human person is a kind of divine art, as creative as the molding of clay or the ordering of words in the writing of a poem. In this process of the person being made Christian, it is the Spirit who is the acting agent of the triune God; for it is the Father who calls and claims us as his children, and the Spirit who seeks to conform us to the image of his Son (Romans 8:29). It is a continuous process, one might almost say a lifelong process, as God seeks to fashion and indeed refashion us each time we distort that image through our sin and self-striving. In this we must let go of the desire "to make something of ourselves" and instead, as the passive form of Paul's vocabulary of salvation verbs suggests, trustingly risk ourselves to the sculpting movement of the Spirit, continuously shaping and reshaping us "till Christ is formed in us" (Galatians 4:19), that is, until the form and shape of Christ is drawn out and made visible in our lives. This vision, of course, presupposes that we ourselves, and the kind of world in which we live, are alert to the signs of the transcendent and open to the transfiguring influence of the Holy Spirit.

At this point, we turn in the next chapter to the witness of some contemporary poetic voices, and see how the experience of lives transformed is also celebrated in the sung poetry of Christian worship.

3

Telling and Showing

As we have seen, the pattern for our being renewed in God's image is drawn in the very witness of the New Testament, and it is precisely this reshaping of the human form to the likeness of Christ that we are calling the art of God. But there is another art form, the art of poetry, that can elicit the transcendent and transforming presence of God. After all, as Augustine said, it is God who is the supreme poet, "the maker of heaven and earth." At the dawn of time, it is God's Word that summons all things into being, forming creation from the formless void: "Let there be . . . and there was" (see Genesis 1). The very utterance of the Word makes that of which it speaks, for it is performative; it literally gives *form* to what it expresses. And this it does because the divine Word is charged with the creative Spirit, the very breath of God: "By the word of the Lord were the heavens made, and the whole host of them by the breath of his mouth (Psalm 33:6; cf. Psalm 104:32). Indeed, so dynamic is the Word of God that it effects what it signifies, and those prophets (see Deuteronomy 18:18f.) who truly voice God's Word, utter an effective Word:

> For as the rain and snow come down from heaven, and do not return there until they have watered the earth, making it bring forth and sprout, giving seed to the sower and bread to the eater, so shall my word be that goes out from my mouth; it shall not return to me empty, but it shall accomplish that which I purpose, and succeed in the thing for which I sent it (Isaiah 55:10–11).

The opening of the Letter to the Hebrews in the New Testament testifies to how God spoke through his servants, the prophets, and declares that God's final and definitive Word appeared with the coming of God's Son (Hebrews 1:1 and 2). This sense of a direct communication between God and humanity, as opposed to inspired speech, echoes the conviction that the Word was made flesh (John 1:14) and suggests that Christ brought the true God to expression to such an extent that Christ himself was the very self-expression of God in embodied form. In John's Gospel, Christ not only reveals God, but is God's self-communication. This is an audacious claim in itself, but there are two further related points in the narrative of John's Gospel that are relevant to our reflections here as to how God brings himself to expression.

First of all, it is significant that the evangelist speaks in almost the same breath of both the words and the works of Jesus, of what he says and what he does. Words and works are closely correlated, almost to the point of being interchangeable. This device of the evangelist underscores both the performative aspect of what Christ says and the fact that what he says is shown in the very physical conditions of our earthly life. Second, in what might well strike the reader as a rather surprising rebuke to his opponents, Jesus says: "You search the scriptures thinking that in them you will find eternal life" (John 5:39). The point drawn by the evangelist in these puzzling words is that Jesus himself embodies in his own person the very word of life.

This apparent distancing between the Word and the words of Scripture should warn us against two prevailing religious attitudes. The first is the kind of biblical literalism which, with its tendency to confine the message to a narrow "religious" meaning, denies all bodily and sensual reference. The second attitude is the kind of moral Pharisaism that, being so intent on hammering home a moral message, flattens out all metaphorical talk of God to the level of the clichéd certainty. It is precisely from such talk that a sense of the poetic can both liberate us and help us to see the texture and tone of our talk of God. The very repetition in the language of praise, "Holy, holy, holy," suggests that the reality of the God of whom we speak evades all adequate verbal description. As the concluding section on transfiguration in the previous chapter suggested, we may be brought to the point where we may see and be shown, but we cannot exactly *say*, what we shall be. Words are simply inadequate to the task: as the poet T. S. Eliot memorably said in the *Four Quartets,* our words strain, break, slip, slide as they bear the freight of meaning in our talk of the things of God.

How are we, then, to find the language? We could begin by drawing a distinction between our talk *about* God and our talking *to* God. Our talking *to* God is the language of prayer, which is always a response to the address of that eternal Word of God, Jesus Christ. Indeed, we could say that our best talk of God is that which is spelled out from the alphabet of prayer, whose characters hint, point to, express, evoke and intentionally invoke that mystery that cannot be contained or caught in the words of human language. So what kind of language; can we possibly use in our worship and our prayer? It is often said that the kind of language we need for worship ought to be poetic language, a language, that is, which is expressive, rhythmic and memorable. It needs to be rhythmic because it needs to move us to a place of encounter with God, and it needs to be expressive to voice the Spirit who prays within us, and make us truly present to the mystery of the divine presence: "when two or three are gathered together in my name." Such language also needs to be direct language, the language of address, as we pray to the Father, through the Son and in the Holy Spirit. And as we approach the triune God, we do not come empty handed, but bring our words; words of praise to express a sense of wonder before the mystery of God and words of penitence to express our sorrow for all that goes wrong in our lives and in our world. For in the speaking of these words of praise and penitence, we realize that relationship with the triune God into which we are drawn by the Spirit, and give voice to that Spirit which prays within us, as brothers and sisters in Christ.

Now the questions of what we might actually say and the kind of hope we might come to articulate are questions that might well be answered if we attend to, and attune our ears to the poetic voice and see what the poet might tell us. For what the poet says can fire our dulled imagination, help us to see things yet unseen, and contribute to a reenchantment of our weary world by showing us the glory of creation and the wonder of being fully alive to the possibilities of change and transformation. The poet, the maker of poems, is a wordsmith who, hammering away in the heat of creativity, attenuates meaning and reconfigures our perceptions of the world through the shaping and stretching of ordinary language. The task of the poet, according to Coleridge, is to find the right words and to place them in the right order so that the poet might convey the deeper reality of an experience to the reader or listener. As with every creative endeavor, this involves a real labor, in this case, a searching for the right words, which cannot simply be plucked from the air. Striking images and metaphors have to be forged which, transcending the flat descriptive language of prose, depict the reality that the poet seeks to encapsulate and convey. Poetry is a precise art, transcribing observation into verbal expression, and requires an economy of expression. As well as being expressive, the language of the poet also has to be evocative and to resonate with the reader's experience. Often the poet will place familiar words in new combinations, make unusual juxtapositions, which surprise the reader into a new or deeper awareness, making the familiar pulsate with meaning. Words will be layered on other words to reinforce an image or to spin further a deliberately figurative form of speech. What is caught in the eventual form of the poem can seem more real than the reality that meets the eye.

The deliberate stretching of language is the function of metaphor, the stock in trade of the poet and those who would speak of the things of God. The word "metaphor" derives from a Greek verb that literally means to throw or carry over the meaning of a word or image from one referent to another, so that on the basis of a perceived similarity or resemblance, "a" is seen as "b." The metaphor does not so much describe as depict, pinpoint and convey the meaning of a word, idea or thing. Much of our everyday talk is metaphorical, where one thing is described in terms of another. Hence we speak of a leg of a table or chair. Such commonplace, everyday language reminds us that over the course of time metaphors can become dull and die, and that is why we need the writing of poets to keep language vitally alive. The newly forged metaphor, of course, can surprise us, and, by triggering the imagination, help us to see even the everyday familiar object or relation in a totally new and fresh light. This is precisely how the similes and parables of Jesus work in the Gospels: "the Kingdom of God is like . . . ." The parable, like the poem, is spun on the basis of a perceived similarity; but every similarity entails an element of dissimilarity and this too can have a positive function in acting as a kind of springboard for the imagination, to help us grasp a deeper and less obvious truth. The parable can become a window on to the transcendent, allowing a new light to illuminate the furniture of our everyday world. On this point we might recall George Herbert's familiar line, "A man that looks on glass, on it may stay his eye, or if he pleaseth, through it pass, and then the heaven espy." Similarly, we might contemplate a Vermeer still-life painting, such as *The Milkmaid* (c. 1657–1658), where a domestic scene is somehow transfigured by the rays of light shining through a window, illuminating and effectively freezing a moment in time as if it were touched by eternity. This is not simply the suspension of time, but a moment in time reverberating with significance. *The Milkmaid* was painted by an artist whose painterly genius lay in revealing the play of natural light on objects, and in this painting Vermeer makes the simple task of pouring milk from a jug appear as a sacramental act, an ordinary human action charged with the beauty and grace of the God who dwells in inaccessible light.

Like the painter of a still-life painting, the poet too needs to be an acutely observant person, one who notices the detail, and who is able to look askance to see how one thing stands in relation to another. In doing these things, the good poet can deepen and extend our field of vision and open up for us new and striking ways of seeing the world, a world which is both a given and something we ourselves make and inhabit. Our perceptions, of course, are crucial. How we *see* things determines to a large extent the ways in which we respond in our thinking, feeling and behavior. In this sense the poet, shaping language on the anvil of experience, cannot only open up for us new ways of seeing, but also extend the possibilities of how we might be in the world. In the poet's seeing and telling of what is, the reader and the world itself seem to be opened up to the possibility of transformation. In a poem entitled "Considerations," the Oxford poet, Elizabeth Jennings, summarizes the transformative effect of poetry in a single, consummate line: "But poetry must change and make / The world seem new in each design."

The making and multiplying of metaphors is the poet's task and one, as Aristotle said, which confers dignity on poetic speech and raises it above the mundane and the commonplace. But Aristotle also warns that art can be illusory and can confuse our perceptions of the real empirical world. As Lewis Carroll's character Alice knew too well, it is only a small step from the world of the imagination to falling into a world of fantasy. Could the kind of world evoked and enlarged by the artist and the poet simply be an illusory chimera, with little or no footing in what we take to be the real world? There is good reason to be wary of the Romantic claim of the poetic genius, which distances the poet from the world that we ordinarily mortals inhabit. But perhaps the most important thing is not to claim for poetry anything that poets do not say or claim for themselves.

In their defense, we might call on two distinguished poets to represent their case. The first, who straddles the worlds of British and American poetry, poet and critic Anne Stevenson, and the second, Seamus Heaney. Anne Stevenson makes the claim in her poem "Alas" that "the way we say the world is what we get." This is a rather startling claim and explodes the received wisdom that how we construe the world and envisage who and what we are is hedged in and bounded by the limitations of what is sayable. Early in his career, the philosopher Ludwig Wittgenstein claimed that the limits of our language are the limits of our world, as if meaningful language was bounded and prescribed by the empirical and predetermined world. But in the very stretching of language through metaphor and evocative speech, the poet demonstrates that language is more pliable and can do more than simply picture things just as they appear to be. It is possible to see things, other people and our relations with them, in new and different lights, and to be surprised by unsuspected and unforeseen possibilities. This, we might say, is the promise held out to us in the work of the poet.

In a poem entitled "Snow," the poet Louis MacNeice tells how the world is "incorrigibly plural," and in claiming that there is "more of it than we think," speaks evocatively of "the drunkenness of things being various." The language here takes us beyond a sense of delight in the created order to a sense of the intoxicating variety of natural life and human culture. The world is pregnant with possibilities and these possibilities invite us into new and different ways of seeing ourselves and of being with and relating to others. It is in this sense that we can hear Anne Stevenson's voice, "the way we say the world is what we get." There are multiple ways of "saying the world," and what we "get of it" depends to a considerable extent on how we tell it. Telling it at a slant might tell more, and the poet's metaphor might well depict an aspect of reality, of which at best we are only vaguely and partially aware. At another level, what Stevenson says is a salutary reminder that we should not see any one single view of the world as the only take on it, and should refuse the claim that any particular account can fully explain who we are and what the world is. The visionary artist and poet, William Blake (1757–1827) protested against the arrogance of those who claimed to give an exhaustive explanation of human life and the world. He claimed to keep "company with angels" and as a proto-Romantic believed that nature offered far more than was accounted for in the reductionist and mechanistic explanations of rationalist philosophers and scientists. Blake celebrated the physicality of the human body-soul, and railed against the "thou shalt not" religious rhetoric and conventional morality of his day, which he felt cramped and corralled the human spirit and imagination (see, for instance, his poem "The Garden of Love" in *Songs of Experience,* 1794). The poet and poetry itself resist such limiting closure, and open up through suggestive imagery and figurative speech a variety of ways of saying how the world is, and of how we might see and actually be in the world. Indeed, the poet often tells of what is generally unseen, and through the lines of a poem leads us to the uncharted depths of existence, and intimates for us a world that is open to the transfiguring touch of the Spirit.

Our second witness is the poet Seamus Heaney who, in his Nobel lecture delivered in 1995, insisted that poetry too was a kind of "truth-telling." The art of poetry, he said, consists in the ordering of words, words that not only convey the impact of the poet's experience of the world, but also ring true to the poet's inner life of sense and feeling. The very form of poetic speech demands a precision in the use of language, and such a verbal economy gives the poem its revelatory aspect, in so far as the well-chosen words and their ordering evocatively depict a place or experience in its distinctive specificity. A striking example of this is Heaney's poem, aptly called "Seeing Things," which in one line conjures up a place called Inish-bofin. The five words he marshals into the second line combine to evoke an experience of a place on a Sunday morning in such a way that one can see, feel and almost smell it: "Sunlight, turfsmoke, seagulls, boatslip, diesel." This superb example illustrates how the poet, in finding and placing the right words in lines of poetry, can give an intensity and depth to the reader's own experience of place and relationships.

There are, of course, different kinds of poetry and different kinds of poet, but generally speaking, the poet's sensibility and feel for the sound and texture of language can give an added depth to our vision, broaden our own horizons, and open up new ways of looking and responding to the world around us. The words of a poem can promise new possibilities, or, indeed, make us think again. Figurative language, far from being a conceit, can also "tell the truth"; and in telling it slant, can lead us to figure it out anew. The truth can be stranger than we might suppose, and by resisting the flat prosaic language of mere description can keep alive that sense of the irreducible mystery of God and the human person.

For the maker of the poem, the words are not always immediately to hand, and sometimes the poet has to wait patiently, with an almost contemplative vigilance, for the right word to suggest itself. This sense of waiting for and struggling to grasp the right word is found even in such an accomplished poet as Kathleen Raine. In her poem "Invocation," Raine sums up the whole creative process in a single line that speaks of the poet seeking to incarnate the spirit. This image of the poet's words being charged with the spirit brings us back to the vocation of the prophet, the one who, like the biblical figure of Jeremiah, is compelled to utter the Word of God.

Originally, the biblical prophet was called "a seer," that is, a person of extraordinary perception, who combined insight with hindsight and foresight. The prophets were clear-eyed, and courageously denounced social injustice and corruption. But even in the steely words of judgment, they also intimated a hope for the future, and sometimes anticipated through prophetic symbolic action what it was that they foretold. The poet Elizabeth Jennings effectively caught the similarities between the prophetic and the poetic vocations in her poem "The Prophets," where she describes the biblical prophets as bearers of God's "early words," the best of which, she says, "make us still," and moreover, "gives grace."

An example of a modern prophetic poet was the American Denise Levertov. Levertov straddled a number of different worlds and drew from a variety of different perspectives. She too, like the eighth-century biblical prophets, was fired by a sense of social justice; she was an anti-Vietnam War protester, a champion of civil rights, and a cultural critic equal to the earlier generation of T. S. Eliot and Ezra Pound. From her own family background Levertov wove together the Eastern European experience of Hasidic Judaism, Welsh Non-Conformity (on her mother's side), and the experience of being brought up in an Anglican vicarage in post-war British society. As a young woman she settled in America, but little from her rich family background was lost in transition. Indeed, her singular power of observation, her remarkable facility for language and her deep religious sensibility reached their zenith with the publication of a collection of poems, *Oblique Prayers*. In this collection, her analysis of the spiritual condition of Western urban society was penetratingly perceptive, and somewhat disconcerting. In her view, for those of us living in a culture driven by endless "buying and spending," there is neither the dark night of the soul, nor the searching light of the desert place in which to unravel our clamoring wants and needs, but instead, a nondescript "gray, a place without clear outlines."

Through her poems, Levertov gives shape to the enigmas of birth, and love, and death, and finely delineates the emotional impact these experiences have upon us. In her work, our experience is not simply reflected back as in a mirror, but rather as in a window, a window through which we might also glimpse new possibilities of being in the world, see new landscapes and social and relational configurations. Her poems speak of the familiar world in a language that makes us look again, and to see in a new light what has become all too familiar, unquestioned, staid or even lackluster. In doing this, Levertov is preeminently a poet of recognition. Her poetry is a celebration of little "epiphanies," in the sense of a showing of what generally goes unnoticed. As such, her work invites us to recognize what is all too frequently unseen and often overlooked. One poem, with the deliberately ambiguous title of "Window Blind," speaks of our inclination to remain blinkered, and tells how we are so often contained by our myopic vision and thereby closed to the possibilities of what might be. Playing with the image of the closing garage door, Levertov exposes our readiness to close down, and to shut off our recognitions. Nevertheless, for those with eyes to see, there are little epiphanies in life, and when they are recognized we can be surprised with the splendor of small revelations. In another poem, aptly named "Something More," Levertov tells how we first need the will "to see more than is there," to be open to seeing more than what immediately meets the eye. If we can be open to such things, then the poem promises those moments when things do register, when we do perceive the more that there is "behind the gray curtains of low expectation." The language here is again the language of revelation, and tells of a recognition of depth and the very splendor of things.

When we experience such moments of recognition, whether it is a matter of recognizing something about ourselves, or noticing a little thing that can give pleasure, like the opening of the first snowdrops presaging the promise of spring, or seeing a smile transform a troubled face, we glimpse an intimation of a world that is open to being transformed. These moments are "graced moments," times when we are reminded that the human frame and the world of nature itself bear the signature of the Creator God. It is as though we glimpse, however fleetingly, that "something more." For some poets, such as Gerard Manley Hopkins, this recognition is an explicitly religious perception, the seeing of world as being charged with the glory of God. Elizabeth Jennings, a more reticent poet, though one who equals Hopkins' religious sensibility, celebrates such an appearing of grace in a tender poem entitled "After Four Months of Illness." This poem includes the gently suggestive line of there being an "invitation in the air." Here the perception of grace, the recognition of moments of epiphany, are not in the arena of brute and incontestable facts, but appear to those with the sensitivity to see and feel Levertov's "more." Elizabeth Jennings, again, speaks of her coming to see her "usual world being lit up anew." This sense of illumination suggests a transfiguration, of the ordinary things being suffused with the radiance of God's grace. Such a poetic perception is reminiscent of the heightened sensitivity often experienced by those emerging from the darkness of depression, when the senses seem to be heightened and the person becomes more aware of the quality of light and color. Such awareness can only be received as gift, as grace, and is well caught by the poet's expression of the world "lit up anew." The dawning of such light often strikes us by surprise, that note of surprise which is so well expressed in the concluding line of Jennings' poem: "Why such a light shines everywhere."

The poem holds out to the reader the familiar world as being reconfigured through figurative speech. It is as though the poet's adjectives can crack open the hardened surface of our mental landscape, and intimate the world in a new light, helping us to see the translucence of things. As Elizabeth Jennings says again, the very form of poetry opens up and invites the reader to see the world transformed, resplendent and redolent with new and latent possibilities. Another modern poetic voice, R. S. Thomas, intimates how the very pace of the language of a poem can, as it were, race ahead of us, catch us out in the contained and controlled worlds we make for ourselves, and confront us, as he puts it in his poem "Arrival," with the one truth that we have everything to look forward to. Such an opening of the future often occurs through a changing encounter with another, in the realization of how we are loved by another, and in those moments when God himself meets us, and we are surprised by the presence of his grace.

But as poets struggle to find the right word in writing their poems, so we too can struggle to find and accept God's grace. Even the religious poet George Herbert (1593–1633), living in a comparatively stable Christian cultural context, articulated in his poetry the stresses, strains and struggles that seem so intrinsic to the Christian being formed into the person he or she is called to be and become. But, paradoxically, it is precisely in those poems, such "The Search," and "The Collar," when Herbert protests at how his knees pierce the earth and his eye vainly searches the heavens, and when he reaches that point where he threatens to abandon the search for God, that a renewed sense of being called and met by God rings in a note of gentle and unexpected assurance of God's grace. Even God's art is a painful labor.

In terms of Christian theology, what makes the world so open to change is the ongoing work of the Creator God, summoning us from the brink of nothingness (see Romans 4:17b) and shaping a creation, so often misshapen by calamity, human brutality and violence, according to the design of the divine will and purpose. The vocation of the poet, rather like that of the priest, is to recognize and to point others to the often imperceptible grace of God; that divine grace that holds everything and everyone in being, and which alone can bring creation to its true fulfillment. For some of us the working of this grace is acknowledged and can be named, but for others, the experience, though equally real, goes unnamed as a trace of an "other." But even such an avowed Christian poet as Gerard Manley Hopkins can evoke the experience of grace, cast it in dense images that reverberate with a multitude of meanings, without explicitly spelling out and naming the subject. Consider, for instance, his poem "As Kingfishers Catch Fire" whose first line signals the traces of Pentecostal fire, without actually mentioning the Holy Spirit. But that the world is illumined and so touched by grace is beyond doubt. Indeed, what might seem to be the reticence of poetic speech might be a salutary warning against domesticating the dynamic operation of God, or of over-subjectifying the experience, as though it were something we might conjure and claim for ourselves. The Spirit blows where it wills. It is the same Spirit who searches the depths, and according to Paul, needs to be interpreted. Perhaps at this point, to use Hopkins' expression, the vocations of the poet and the priest coincide in seeking to give voice to the "deep down things."

In a poem entitled "The Minister," describing a funeral of a friend in north Wales, Anne Stevenson says that we need the minister to "take care of the words." The best a minister can do is to testify to the visible effects of the Spirit, and help us figure out those graced moments in life, those beginnings and ends, and the repeated new beginnings in our lives. Although it is distinctively the priest who invokes the sacred name in blessing, the poet often evokes the presence of that Spirit which is as invisible as the air in the wind. One might think of Christiania Whitehead's poem, "Deer at Dawn," where she speaks of the Spirit as the piercing new light of dawn, claiming anew the world as God's creation and as reflecting his glory: "The sunlight, still slippered, / shone inside each leaf, illuminating / and connecting the glory to the glory." The language in this poem is so simple, and yet so directly evocative and theologically suggestive, that it is reminiscent of Hopkins' celebrated poems of praise, such as "Hurrahing in Harvest" and "Pied Beauty," which praises the Creator "for dappled things." A sense of the presence of God immanent in his creation, through the Spirit, underwrites the simple evocative lines of the poet.

But what of God's redemptive work, of the necessary reworking of creation, the renewal of humanity disfigured by brutality, numbed by calamity and, to use Hopkins' description, "bleared, smeared with toil"? Can the evocative language of the poet also invoke the redeeming Spirit, the liberating Spirit that reveals the children of God and releases creation from its bondage to decay? There is a sense of the contingent, physical world looking to humankind for its redemption and this is certainly sounded by the German poet, Rilke. In one poem, the "Ninth Duino Elegy," he suggests that the world looks to be taken into us, and thereby transformed, looks to us to be changed, and so he rhetorically asks if the earth seeks to be raised up in us. The natural world of creation itself yearns for its redemption, and looks for the revealing of God's children and our bodily redemption (see Romans 8:20–23) that is anticipated in every celebration of the Eucharist. As Irenaeus said, the bread and wine brought for the Eucharist is an offering of the first-fruits of creation, and so, at the presentation of the gifts of bread and wine at the celebration of the Eucharist we can pray: "Blessed are you, Lord God of all creation, of your goodness we have these gifts to offer, fruit of the earth . . . and work of human hands . . . they shall become the bread of life and the cup of salvation." The words of this prayer not only point ahead to the gifts of Communion, but also intimate how the elements of the created natural world are taken up and redeemed in the celebration of the Eucharist.

When the apostle Paul speaks of creation as being "in travail" (Romans 8:22), he casts the Spirit in the role of a midwife bringing a new world to birth. In the 1662 Book of Common Prayer this passage was appointed to be read as the Epistle at the celebration of Holy Communion on the fourth Sunday after Trinity, and in John Keble's poem in The Christian Year to mark this Sunday in the Church's calendar, he presents a sacramental view of the world, telling how even the "meanest" of earthly life can be purged and restored to its pristine form by the heavenly fire of the Spirit:

> Thenceforth, to eyes of high desire.
> The meanest things below,
> As with a Seraph's robe of fire
> Invested, burn and glow.
>
> "Trinity IV"

The use of the verb "burn" derives from the metaphor of the Spirit as fire, and depicts the purgative, or purifying influence of the Spirit upon us. This purging work of the Spirit on the human form is like the removal of corrosive rust and the polishing of tarnished silver, so that the Christian might reflect more brilliantly the glow of the divine indwelling grace of God. The purgative effect of divine visitation, of our being touched by the cleansing hand of God, was a frequent theme in the sacred poetry of John Donne (1572–1631). This is most obviously seen in his poem "Goodfriday, 1613. Riding Westward." In this poem Donne honestly admits the difficulty of facing the contorted figure of the crucified Christ, but the difficulty is finally resolved in the recognition of the working of divine grace, leading the penitent to ask: "Burn off my rusts, and my deformity, / Restore thine Image, so much, by thy grace, / That thou mayest know mee, and I'll turn my face." In the end, the Christian, like Donne, can face the dying Christ because we ourselves have been faced by God in the incarnation. For through the child born of Mary the image of God, burnished and tarnished in us, is seen in its pristine fullness.

In his earlier profane poetry, Donne had artfully interwoven the sensual with the sacramental, and brought both these dimensions into a mutually illuminating relationship with each other. Similarly, in his later sacred poems Donne fully reconciled the outward ceremony of public liturgy with the inward working of God's grace. In his verse, as in his later sermons, the sacramental language of traditional scholastic and Tridentine theology is often recast, and its meaning subverted and reappropriated. In one Christmas sermon on the incarnation, for instance, Donne takes the very term that had dogged the doctrinal controversies of the Reformation, and speaks of the communicants themselves, rather than the elements of bread and wine, as being "transubstantiated," of being Christ. By ingesting the sacramental body and blood of Christ, the communicant becomes Christ (see Christmas Sermon, 1626).

Donne's treatment of the theme of the restoring of the divine image and the transforming of the communicant recalls the tension that St. Augustine of Hippo experienced in himself, that contradiction he recognized himself to be, unChristlike, and yet at one and the same time, glowing with Christlikeness. In one aspect he was unlike Christ, and yet in his loving relationships was Christ for others. In his *Confessions,* Augustine expresses the tension in his typically intensely personal way: "I am overwhelmed by the measure that I am unlike him; I glow with fire in the measure that I am like him." The tension is finally resolved in Augustine's understanding of the second and glorious coming of Christ at the end of time and human history.

In the present, though, the Christian can even now reflect, however imperfectly or momentarily, something of the divine glory through his or her encounter with the Christ who constantly looks on us with his mercy and grace. Rather like the blush on the face of lovers after they have furtively caught each other's eye, the Christian too can catch the radiant glory of the face of the divine countenance that constantly gazes upon us, his beloved sons and daughters. The effect of our being held and transfigured in the transforming radiance of Christ's gracious countenance is tenderly expressed again by Keble:

But with mild radiance every hour,
From our dear Saviour's face benign
Bent on us with transforming power,
Till we, too, faintly shine.

As an art form, poetry is closest to music, the art of marking sound in time. Like the musician or composer, the poet has an ear for rhythm, pace, sound and silence, and modulates the voice to catch the whole range of human sense and feeling. The ancient chant of the Church, both Western Gregorian chant, and the Eastern Byzantine chant, works in tandem with the libretto of worship and lifts the meaning, as it were, from the written text, so that the meaning is sounded. Singing the Word is a thoroughly physiological act, involving the use of lungs and diaphragm, as well as tongue and teeth in the enunciation of words. Singing widens the tonal range beyond that of ordinary speech, and so again heightens the sense of the physical body being engaged in worship. It involves, we might say, the whole of the person, the mind as well as the body. As St. Benedict directs in his *Rule,* when the monk sings in church, his mind has to be in harmony with his voice. Benedict, of course, would have known the saying of Augustine of Hippo that the person who sings prays twice. Singing, we might say, can enhance prayer and through the act of singing the sense of what is sung can be incarnated in the person who prays.

The bringing together of words and melody, the blending of words and music in song, is most commonly seen in the tradition of hymnody. Ancient hymns, such as those attributed to St. Ambrose, are dense with biblical allusions, and consummately set the tone and mood of a particular liturgical season, or the character of the day's commemoration. Hymnody, of course, was revived at the Reformation, classically in compositions such as *Ein Feste Burg* by the German Reformer, Martin Luther, and was a form adopted by seventeenth-century English divines as diverse as the Puritan pastor Richard Baxter and the High Churchman Thomas Ken. Hymnody became a prominent vehicle of Christian piety in the eighteenth-century with the emergence of Methodism and the subsequent Evangelical and Catholic revivals of the nineteenth century in the Church of England. The repertoire expanded still further in the twentieth century, but it would seem that still more needs to be done to help clergy and congregations see that hymnody and music as a whole are an integral element to the transformative worship of the Church, and not simply a filler between the seemingly more important bits of what is said and done in church when Christians gather for worship.

The great nineteenth-century Danish theologian Nikolai Grundtvig (1783–1872) was a prolific hymnwriter, and once declared in a Christmas sermon that sound was the very life of the Word, suggesting that rhythm itself was the impulse of the Holy Spirit (see Watson, 1997, p. 23). The mystery of the living God eludes our neat logical categories and chiseled moral certainties, and yet finds expression in the songs of those who, like Grundtvig, know the grace of God which meets us in our own personal suffering and struggle with the riddle of love (see Stevenson, 1996, Chapter 6). The Creator's gift of the breath of life to humankind is destined to be given back to the Creator in a song of praise (see Psalm 150; Revelation 14:3).

Charles Wesley, the co-founder of Methodism with his brother John, remained a priest of the Church of England until his death and must surely rank as the most accomplished writer in the modern history of hymnody. Methodism, as is often said, was born in song. Charles Wesley's writing, although close to the genre of English lyric poetry associated with John Donne and George Herbert, was cast in the form of hymnody, the literary form of verse that some have considered to be poetry's poor relation. But we need to remember that the verses of hymns are crafted to be sung, and thereby overcome what T. S. Eliot described as the dissociation of sensibility by appealing to both the head and the heart. Of course hymn-singing was well suited to kindling that expression of Christianity which set such a high premium upon the religious experience of the individual, and which had recovered a sense of the individual's sanctification, alongside the Reformation emphasis upon "justification by grace through faith alone." The very practice of Christianity, what the Wesley brothers referred to as "experimental religion," was grounded on the double doctrinal tracks of justification and sanctification. The two doctrines were regarded as being inextricably linked, and in one of his dense expository sermons, John Wesley spelled how justification was God's saving act *for* us, whereas Sanctification was God's saving act *in* us. The first, he said, removes guilt, the second removes sin; and again, the first restores us to favor, the other, he said, restores in us the image of God (*Works,* Vol. V. *Sermon XIX,* cited by Whaling, 1981, p. 48). This hope of being restored in the image of God is a frequent and repeated theme in Charles Wesley's hymns. The first published collection, consisting of 166 hymns, was published in 1745.

As we read the hymns of Charles Wesley we soon become aware of a distinct axis between incarnation and participation, of God becoming enfleshed in Jesus Christ and of the Christian sharing in the enlivening Spirit of God. In one Christmas hymn, for instance, Wesley affirms the incarnation, of how "Our God contracted to a span" and is "Incomprehensibly made man," in order that God might "make us all divine." This sense of "divination," of our sharing the very life of God, finds its most explicit celebration in the third stanza of the hymn "Seeking for Full Redemption." This hymn includes the lines "Heavenly Adam, Life divine, / Change my nature into thine." The change that is asked and hoped for is nothing less than our transformation that is understood to be the work of the Holy Spirit, the operation of divine grace, of whom our very physical body is the temple. Thus, Wesley could speak of the indwelling Holy Spirit. Further, it was the indwelling Spirit that was regarded as the transfiguring presence of God, leading Charles Wesley to allude, as he frequently did in his verses, to the radiancy of the Spirit shining in the life of the Christian. In his morning hymn, "Christ whose Glory Fills the Skies" we find, for instance, the line "Fill me, radiancy divine." Again, the source of such radiance is named in the fourth stanza of the hymn "Come, Holy Ghost, our Hearts Inspire," and its effect indicated in the lines: "God, through himself, we then shall know, / If thou within us shine." Indeed, Charles' hymns repeatedly invoke the Spirit, and one gathering hymn, "Ye Simple Souls that Stray", designated for Sunday morning, asks that worshippers may be "filled with the life of God". Undoubtedly the most well-known and frequently sung of Wesley's hymns, "Love Divine, All Loves Excelling," celebrates the Holy Spirit and voices the same hope of transformation in the phrase: "changed from glory into glory." It is not surprising, then, to find that a good number of Charles Wesley's Whit Sunday hymns, published in 1746, celebrate this transforming work of the Holy Spirit.

In presenting the classical understanding of humanity created in the "image of God" in his verse, Wesley also recognized that living in the kind of world in which our lives are set that image is all too often marred and disfigured by sin. In order to show the lines of the divine impress, the stamp of our divine maker, humankind needs to be reshaped and refashioned. Hence in the original form of the hymn "Hark How All the Welkin Rings," Wesley included the stanza:

Adam's likeness, Lord efface,
Stamp thy image in its place.
Second Adam from above
Reinstate us in thy love.

And in a further stanza, the Lord is asked to come and restore nature defaced by human violence and sin:

Come, desire of nations, come
Ruined nature now restore.

Indeed, the making and remaking of humanity after the pattern of Christ and through the operation of the Holy Spirit provides the unifying theme throughout the collections of Wesley's hymns, which originally extended and complemented the liturgical forms of public prayer provided in The Book of Common Prayer. Alongside the provision of morning and evening prayer in the Prayer Book was, of course, the celebration of the sacrament of Holy Communion, that singular celebrated "means of grace." John Wesley's defense of Christianity as a sacramental religion was pronounced, and he seized upon hymnody as a means of enriching the official authorized liturgy of the English Church. Indeed, his collection of eucharistic hymns gave voice to those elements of eucharistic theology which, in the 1662 Prayer Book "Order of the Holy Communion were muted, if not totally absent. After the opening prayer, "Almighty God unto whom all hearts be open . . . ." in the Prayer Book service, for instance, there is no further reference to the Holy Spirit. The eucharistic hymns would provide what was lacking in the liturgical form of service. In one of Wesley's Communion hymns, the Spirit's work is described as a "heavenly art," making the elements of bread and wine effectual signs and "channels to convey Thy love" *(Hymns for the Lord's Supper of 1745, 72)*. As a channel of grace, the Communion was regarded by Wesley as a real participation in the very life of God, and this was the mystery of the Eucharist, that in and through Communion "God into man conveys" (57). Furthermore, this sharing in the life of God through Communion was also the means whereby the communicant might be shaped more clearly into the likeness of Christ. Thus, the final stanza of the hymn "Lamb of God" asks that through Communion God would "Write forgiveness on our heart, / and all thy image give!"

In a similar vein, another of Wesley's Communion hymns expresses the hope that the communicants themselves might feel the weight of Christ's "heavenly impress." The underlying image in this condensed metaphor is that of a mold being pressed into soft wax and leaving its exact pattern and shape, and gives rise to the repeated image of the "stamp" in Wesley's verses. The effect of sanctifying grace, that divine gift of love in which the Christian is being perfected, stamps afresh the divine image upon us: "Love, thine image, love impart! / Stamp it on our face and heart." The very physicality of the language used here resists a limited reading of an interior religious feeling, and speaks rather of the whole person being changed and shaped by God: "let me *all* thy stamp receive." Every aspect of our being, in other words—the physical, mental and emotional—are to be wholly molded by the divine love until "We bear the character divine, / The stamp of perfect love." The language here is reminiscent of John Donne, who in his *Divine Meditations* spoke of the generosity of the Creator God in making humankind in the divine image. But this divine self-giving was seen to be even greater in the event of the incarnation: "Twas much that man was made like God before, / But that God should be made like man, much more" (15). The superfluity of the divine self-giving overflowed and became the means of the Christian's adoption as a son or daughter of God: "I am thy son, made with thy self to shine . . . thy image." (2). And all this, as Donne says in his "To Mr. Tilman after he had taken orders," was considered to be the work of God's Spirit, who is both the divine giver and the gift: "so hath grace / changed only God's old image by creation, / to Christ's new stamp. . . ."

In the first chapter we registered the ambiguity of the biblical language of image and likeness, and introduced the distinction drawn by Irenaeus between our being created according to God's image and our growing into the divine likeness. In the repository of Christian hymnody, the term "image" generally belongs to the vocabulary of creation, and the term "likeness" to the vocabulary of redemption, as these related themes are celebrated in the turning cycles of the Christian year, marking out in times and seasons the Christian story of salvation. Thus some of the ancient hymns, composed to be sung during the Church's offering of prayer and praise, morning and evening, such as those attributed to Prudentius (348–413) and Venantius Fortunatus (530–609), tell of the creation of humankind as the revealing of the divine image and of the Fall as the obscuring and impairing of that image. In Christmas hymnody, the birth of the Christ child is seen as the appearing in visible form of the invisible God, the repristinization of the divine image, which is then restored in humankind through the paschal mystery of Christ's death and resurrection. The hymns for Pentecost, the fulfillment of the Easter season, celebrate in song the sending of the Spirit by the Father to refresh, restore and renew individual Christians in the divine likeness of that humanity, that even now is glorified in the humanity of the ascended Christ. The singing of hymnody through the Christian year can then also have a formative effect; in the physical act of singing what we voice is "written on the body," as one Victorian hymn writer, William Romanis (1824–1899), expressed it: "O Jesus form within us / Thy likeness clear and true" (from his hymn: "Lord, Who Shall Sit Beside Thee?").

If God is, as Augustine said, the quintessential poet, then those who bear his stamp and signature reveal the very form of his making. The poetic form of our being made into the likeness of Christ finds expression in the language of worship, and so it is this aspect of God's art, the language of the liturgy, of what should be the Church's poetry, to which we now turn our attention.

4

Liturgical Reform and the Formation of Christians

It has been said that more liturgical texts have been written and authorized for use by the mainstream Christian Churches during the last 25 years than in any previous period of Christian history. To the writing of liturgical texts there is no end, and from a situation where most of us had one single book, with a small collection of resource books with appropriate material for the seasons of the Christian year, we now have a whole library of different books. But the real revolution in liturgical revision has been a technical one with the arrival of easily accessible worship texts on a plethora of web sites, and the publication of official computer programs such as *Visual Liturgy*, which allows us to "cut and paste" to produce a liturgy tailor-made for our local community and congregation. The scope this gives to local worshipping communities to frame orders of worship adapted to the needs and resources of a particular setting is largely welcome. But what are the risks? The first is the tension and inevitable disparity between the local and the universal, the parochial and the national, which could fuel the drive towards a narrow parochialism and an increasing "congregationalism" within the Church of England. The proliferation of available texts, options and alternatives literally numbering in the thousands makes for an extraordinary consumerist approach to liturgy in which we compile our own orders of service and develop our own style of worship.

Some lament the erosion of even a semblance of *common* worship, and the passing of even a shared family likeness. Others rightly point out that worship is much more than the reading and singing of texts, and draw attention to how an act of worship might be celebrated in the setting in which it takes place. The more cautious question is whether, even with the convenience of computer liturgy, we actually have the competence to shape the worship of the worshipping communities of which we are a part. Have so-called "worship leaders" received an adequate grounding in liturgical education and formation? These are real and very pressing questions. But the debate needs to be wider, and faced with the ever-expanding industry of liturgical revision and the prodigious publication of new materials and resources, we perhaps need to recall that the impetus for liturgical renewal in the mainstream churches arose out of a perceived need to renew the worshipping life of the churches. This was not a call for relevance or accessibility, but a desire to return to the roots that might feed and nourish us in the actual living out of Christian life in the social and economic conditions of everyday life. The book that caught the moment of liturgical renewal more than any other was Gabriel Hebert's *Liturgy and Society* first published in 1935. Rather significantly, the subtitle was "The Function of the Church in the Modern World," and a glance at the index reveals that the foci of interest cluster around the themes of the Church as the Body of Christ, the Eucharist and the Incarnation. Worship is presented as the definitive activity of the Church and the source of Christian life that is to flow across the whole gamut of quotidian activity and thereby extend God's incarnation in human history and society.

Of course, Hebert's book is a book of its own time, and we must look at how the agenda of liturgical renewal entered the modern Church of the West. The great watershed for Roman Catholics was the Second Vatican Council (1962–1965) whose document *Sacrosanctum Concilium* endorsed the aims of the twentieth-century liturgical movement and mandated the revision of the liturgy. This document spelled out the aims of liturgical renewal, the first of which was to enable a conscious and active participation of the faithful in the Church's worship. People had to be enabled to understand what they did, said and heard when they gathered with fellow Christians for worship. Hence the need for worship in the vernacular, or as Cranmer insisted at the time of the English Reformation, in a tongue "understanded of the people. "Questions of comprehensibility inevitably led to questions of culture, and the recognition that different peoples have a distinctive cultural genius. The Christian faith, which was taken to be primarily expressed in the forms of Christian worship, needed to be translated into a variety of cultural contexts.

What might work for Christians in Milan would not work for the people of the Masai. It is not only a stock of words to be translated, but customs, local dress, symbols and styles of worship. The totality of these factors amounts to celebration, and the driving motivation was the need for Christians to be sufficiently formed liturgically to enable them to participate more fully in the celebration of Christian worship. The catch phrase of "active participation" led to the coining of the expression "liturgical formation." But what is meant by this term? There are, of course, various ways of spelling this out, and how we account for it will, in part, be determined by the presuppositions that we bring to a consideration of the vital task of liturgical formation.

In order to clarify how the task and aims of liturgical formation might be viewed, I have grouped three sets of presuppositions, or approaches (none of which is mutually exclusive, and each equally valid and important in its own right), arranged under three rather loose general headings:

The liberal The liberal approach relates back to the didactic emphasis of the English Prayer Book tradition, but sees education as being one of the key aims of corporate worship, and the drawing out of the responsible Christian person as its goal. In this case, rationality is highly prized, making explanations the means of formation and the desired outcome—informed worshippers who have a greater confidence and understanding of what it is that they are asked to say and sing and do when they gather in church for worship. Proponents of this view would promote the kind of "informed participation" that would facilitate an intelligent engagement on the part of the worshipper, and a deliberate linking of the wider experiences of life and worship itself.

The evangelical The evangelical dimension focuses upon the gathering of people before and under the Word of God in order that they might be convinced and converted by the Gospel of Christ. In this view, worship is primarily the occasion for proclamation and preaching. Those concerned with formation would want to see a more biblically literate and personally committed congregation, and would seek to achieve this through smaller house groups as well as through teaching opportunities in worship itself. The evangelical approach would tend towards the didactic, and some of the likely key terms one would find in its discourse would be "teach," "live out" and "service."

The sacramental In continuity with the tradition of Caroline Divines and the nineteenth-century Catholic revival, this approach would give centrality to the celebration of the sacraments, and place an emphasis upon the transcendent mystery of worship in which the divine presence is accorded a degree of objectivity. Liturgical actions would be regarded as "performative acts," and the very occasion of worship as the locus for the formation of the Christian in the likeness of Christ. An articulation of this view of formation would employ more organic terms such as "grow," "nurture" and "form."

Despite the differing approaches reflected in these three models, it is my contention that a notion of formation is explicit in the very language of our worship, and it is to this that we turn. In this chapter I particularly want to examine recent liturgical writing and to trace out how a sense of liturgical formation is found in the very vocabulary and grammar of the liturgical texts themselves. The focus of my inquiry is on recent Church of England liturgical texts that I have examined by applying a method of linguistic and historical analysis. This analysis has yielded a whole cluster of terms and expressions, which I have styled "formational vocabulary." My intention here is to demonstrate that "formation" has emerged as a major theme in contemporary Church of England liturgical revision, to trace its provenance, to locate the discourse culturally, and to offer some reflections as to how we might more fully understand how such language works.

The provenance of formation language

First, where does such language actually come from? The language of our being made in the image of God and remade in the likeness of Christ is embedded in the traditions of baptismal liturgies, in the rites of baptism belonging to the Eastern, Oriental and Western churches. Echoes are also found in the fourth-century catechetical lectures given to those preparing for baptism in Antioch and Jerusalem. But as our concern is with liturgical language, we will focus on the texts of the liturgical rites themselves. These rites, from the ancient through the medieval to those in use on the eve of the English Reformation, are charted in Maxwell Johnson's new edition of *The Documents of Baptismal Liturgy* (2003).

An ancient prayer for the blessing of the water in the Egyptian *Sacramentary of Serapion* (probably mid-fourth century) actually uses the term "form" and its cognates in a petition asking that those to be baptized might be formed according to the divine form and that being "re-formed and born again they may be able to be saved and counted worthy of your Kingdom." A Western variant, the eighth-century *Gelasian Sacramentary*, included the following petition in the prayer of blessing over the font: "Here may the nature which was founded upon your image be restored to the honor of its origin." Similarly, a tenth-century liturgical manuscript *The Ambrosian Manual*, probably reflecting liturgical expressions of a much earlier period in Milan, included a petition that God would "restore the innocence which Adam lost in paradise," and explicitly asked that those to be baptized might "receive the likeness of God." In a prayer for the candidates to be baptized in the rite of the Syrian Orthodox Church of Antioch, we find the exquisite line asking that God would "stamp and impress" on the baptized "the image of your Christ." In the prayer for the blessing of the water for baptism, following an extended and elaborate invocation of the Holy Spirit, we find the petition that the baptized might be "renewed by the image of the Creator," which seems to have been a fairly universal petition. Thus a petition asking that those being baptized may be "refashioned" and "restored after the image of the Creator" occurs in the prayer for the blessing of the water in the Byzantine rite, which we might take as representing the understanding of the Eastern Church generally. Vestiges of this formational turn of liturgical language are found in later and other regional rites of the Western Church, such as those that were used in France, Ireland and Spain. One formula, from an eleventh-century Spanish liturgical book compiled for the use of a bishop, echoed the earlier Ambrosian (Milanese rite) and asked that the baptized may "receive the likeness of God" (*The Liber Ordinum*, 1052). Right up to the eve of the Reformation in England, prayers for the blessing of the water for baptism retained this "formational vocabulary," and a petition in the Sarum (Salisbury) baptismal rite, again following an invocation of the Holy Spirit upon the water, asked that those being baptized in it might be renewed in the divine image in which they were created.

The story of the appropriation of formation language into a eucharistic context is a fascinating conundrum. Historically, as illustrated above, the language of the Christian being renewed in God's image and conformed to Christ generally belonged to the vocabulary of baptism, but it was not totally unknown in a eucharistic context. Such language is found in the *Anaphora* (Eucharistic Prayer) in the Syrian liturgical tradition, the so-called Liturgy of St. James, associated with the ancient Church in Jerusalem, and used in the contemporary Christian world, most notably by the Syrian Orthodox Church in India. A particular feature of the Liturgy of St. James is the full rehearsal of the story of salvation in the first half of the Eucharistic Prayer. After the Sanctus, the "Holy, holy, holy," the narrative rehearses the saving work of Christ, and in both the Syriac and Greek versions of the Liturgy accounts for Christ's coming in terms of the renewal of the divine image in humankind, which the Syriac version says was "worn out." The Liturgy of St. James has attracted the attention of Anglicans, not least through Bishop Jeremy Taylor's *A Communion Office,* privately published as part of his *Collection of Offices* in 1658. The use of the Prayer Book, of course, was forbidden throughout the time of Cromwell's Long Parliament, following the Civil War. In compiling his *Communion Office,* Taylor (1613–1667) drew heavily on the Liturgy of St. James, which he claimed "makes better fuel for the fires of devotion" than the Puritan's *Westminster Directory.* The *Directory* reflected the mainstream Reformed Calvinism of the time, and was summarily dismissed by Taylor as straw and stubble hurriedly raked together. In his translation of the Greek version of the Liturgy of St. James, Taylor gives us the fine phrase about Christ being sent into the world to "renew and repair Thy broken image." Another notable example of the influence of the ancient Liturgy of Jerusalem is seen in the liturgical work of the Scottish bishop, Thomas Rattray (1684–1743), whose rather idiosyncratic compilation and translation of the Liturgy was published by a group of his admirers in London a year after his death. Rattray claimed that the Liturgy of St. James represented a "marriage of East and West," and he reveled in the full recital of God's work of creation and redemption in the narrative sweep of its Eucharistic Prayer.

Although the theme of creation, let alone recreation in the likeness of Christ, is muted in the official Church of England's Order of Holy Communion in The Book of Common Prayer, traces of the theme are found in the writing of those Anglican Divines who shaped the identity of the established English Church and provided points for its theological self-understanding. In this respect, one might cite the literary work of Richard Hooker (1554–1600) and Bishop Lancelot Andrewes (1555–1626). In Book V of his *Of the Laws of Ecclesiastical Polity,* setting out a rationale for the national established Church as a liturgical church against the protest of the Puritans, Hooker describes the Communion in terms of gift, and highlights its transformative effect. When we receive the gift and grace of Holy Communion, Hooker claimed, God "truly conformeth us into the image of Jesus Christ." In a similar vein, in a sermon for the Feast of Pentecost, Lancelot Andrewes spoke of how grace was imparted in the eucharistic gifts of Christ's body and blood to effect "the renewing in us (of) the image of God whereunto we are created" (as noted by F. E. Brightman in his 1903 edition of Lancelot Andrewes' *The Preces Privatae*, p. 122). Although the cause and manner of Christ's sacramental presence tended to be treated somewhat circumspectly by sixteenth-century Anglican Divines, the effects of receiving the grace and gift of Holy Communion seems, on the contrary, to have been spelled out more directly and with conviction in terms of the formation of the faithful communicant.

So much for the history. What of our present forms of service? Those accustomed to using the Order One of the Church of England's *Common Worship* Eucharist will be familiar with the petition, following the *epiclesis*, an invocation of the Holy Spirit: "form us in the likeness of Christ." The story of the origin of this phrase and its inclusion in contemporary Eucharistic Prayers belongs to an interesting episode in the story of recent liturgical revision by the Church of England. The phrase is not found in the liturgical revisions of the 1960s and early 1970s (Series 1, 2 and 3, respectively), and was first tabled by George Timms, then Archdeacon of Hackney, at a meeting of a General Synod Revision Committee reviewing the draft Eucharistic Prayers for the proposed Alternative Service Book (ASB). Timms' memorandum contained a whole new section of prayer, to follow the *anamnesis* (the memorial of Christ), including a petition that the communicants might "grow in his (Christ's) likeness." The Standing Committee were reluctant to accept Timms' emendation on the grounds that the Liturgical Commission had already agreed to preclude any intercessory type of prayer in the Eucharistic Prayer itself. The expression Timms had framed about the communicant being shaped more closely to the image of Christ, evidently encapsulated his understanding of the benefits of Communion, and found its way into his Communion hymn "Blessed Jesus, Mary's Son" (275 in *The New English Hymnal*, 1986, of which, incidentally, Timms was the chief editor). In the second verse of the hymn we find the line ". . . through these gifts of bread and wine / Thine own image in us fashion" which explicitly makes the point. But resuming the story of the genesis of the ASB, a Revision Committee meeting at the end of 1978 retrieved Timms' Christlikeness phrase and inserted it in the prayer that became the Second Eucharistic Prayer of the ASB Rite A, Order of Holy Communion. The phrase also found its way into "A Eucharistic Prayer for Use with the Sick" in *The Alternative Service Book 1980.* The exact phrasing, following the *anamnesis,* is cast in a purposive clause specifying the "benefits" of Communion, and elides the images of sacramental feeding and the communicant's growth in Christlikeness:

> as we eat and drink these holy gifts . . .
> nourish us with the body and blood of your Son,
> that we may grow into his likeness . . .
>
> ASB Rite A, EP2, and EP for Use with the Sick

This phrasing has had some influence on the framing of other Eucharistic Prayers in the wider Anglican Communion, particularly the First Eucharistic Prayer in the Prayer Book of the Province of Southern Africa, published in 1989, which in the concluding paragraph asks that "we may daily grow into his likeness." But an assured place in the Eucharist Prayers for the Church of England's "liturgy 2000" was uncertain. The expression was not used in any of the six Eucharist Prayers originally proposed for *Common Worship.* As it happened, these six prayers were rejected by a newly elected General Synod in 1996. The outcome was that a number of new Eucharistic Prayers had to be drafted. The first conflated the First and Second Eucharistic Prayers in the ASB in such a way that the phrase "grow into his likeness" in Prayer 2 was lost. But the phrase had evidently so impressed itself upon the liturgical memory that the Church of England Liturgical Commission were keen to retain it, and so the phrase "form us into the likeness of Christ" found its way into two of the six Eucharistic Prayers (F and G) in Order One of the Holy Communion in *Common Worship* (2000).

The prevalence of formational language, of our being formed and remade after Christ's likeness, is a significant linguistic phenomenon in recent Church of England, and wider Anglican, liturgical revision. Examples are diverse and can be found in the recent publication of collects by the Church of Ireland, and in the prayer of confession in the Kenyan Liturgy, regarded by many as a good example of inculturated liturgy. The prevalence of formational language in authorized liturgical material for the Church of England is noticeably marked, and given the increased frequency of its use, it could well be taken as a particular characteristic of *Liturgy 2000.*

The analysis of formational language

The prevalence and comprehensive spread of formational language across different kinds of liturgical material, sacramental rites, seasonal material, services of the Word, pastoral offices such as funerals, and ordination rites is demonstrated when the liturgical material is analyzed generically as follows:

Generic classification

Sacramental
(baptismal; Eucharist; oils for anointing, ordination)

Prayers
(collects; post Communion)

Prayers of the people
(intercessory formula; general confessions, etc.)

Presidential declarations
(blessings; absolution formula, etc.)

An analysis of the vocabulary used to articulate this theme in liturgical rites reveals a preponderance of verbs, or "doing words," and pans out thus:

Verbs	Nouns
change	glory
conform	image
create/make	likeness
form	life
fashion	pattern
grow	splendor
partake	
refashion	

reflect
renew
restore
reveal
shine
strengthen
transform

The preponderance of verbs in this word-field (where God, in Christ and through the Spirit, is the acting subject) is indicative that something is sought, of an expectation that something will happen as Christians gather consciously before the presence of the triune God in worship. The use of the language itself reflects an increasing understanding of what might be styled as the performative effect of worship, namely that in an act of worship something happens beyond the observable and recordable realm of speech, song and ritual gesture. Although the theme is not discussed in any official reports or commentary on *Common Worship*, the language of the worship texts themselves reflects an implicit understanding of corporate worship as the performative act in which the worshipper, in community with others, is transformed into the likeness of Christ. Whether such an "official" or even "public meaning," to use the Jewish liturgical scholar Lawrence A. Hoffman's scale of meanings, corresponds to the "public meaning" and extends to the "private meanings" of individual worshippers is a crucial point, but one beyond the scope of this chapter which aims to reveal the shift towards a formational model of worship and to elucidate its meaning.

Having identified the vocabulary of formational language, one might also look at its distribution in a thematic way. Such a thematic analysis reveals a connection between what is sought, and when. The tracing of such connections shows a linkage between the expressed outcome and the different seasons of the Christian year or occasion being celebrated, whether in a sacramental or a pastoral rite.

Thematic analysis

(a) Themes and seasonal time

(1) Themes of "creating" and "making" occur in the seasonal material for both the festive cycles of Christmas and Easter.

(2) Theme of "remaking" occurs in both Advent and Lent.
(3) Theme of "strengthen" occurs in material for Lent and Transfiguration.

(b) Themes and occasions

(1) Theme of human beings created in the imago Dei in **pastoral** rites for marriage and funerals.
(2) Link between **baptism** and the renewal of the imago Dei.
(3) Connection between the shaping of Christlikeness and participation in the **Eucharist.**

The thematic range and its vocabulary

A double-entry system of logging instances of the use of formational vocabulary in recent Church of England and wider Anglican liturgical revision reveals a significant degree of thematic linkage and cross-matching across the liturgical seasons of the Christian year. One obvious and predictable example is the linkage between the Feast of the Transfiguration (August 6) and the Epiphany season, which hinges on the category of "transformation." But other cross-matches can also be made: for example, a comparative reading of the theme of transformation in this material shows that the key term "glory" operates as a correlative term of both transformative cause and effect. Further textual analysis reveals that terms related in the vocabulary of transfiguration (such as "shine," "radiance," "illumine," "light") link across the seasons of the Christian year from All Saints through to Trinity Sunday.

So far, our analysis reveals a rich pattern of linkage across themes and seasons of the Christian year, and is written into different kinds of liturgical celebrations, whether of the Word, sacramental or pastoral rites. In each case, the relationship hinges upon some aspect of the drama of salvation, of what God in Christ offers and brings to humanity, and what is recognized as being needed or asked for by those who on a given time and occasion gather and invoke the divine presence in the act of worship. The vocabulary, as we have seen, is dynamic and presupposes a correlation between the divine presence that is both promised and invoked and its effect on those who pray that God may fashion his Church to be the Body of Christ. The correlation is best shown diagramatically as in Figure 2.

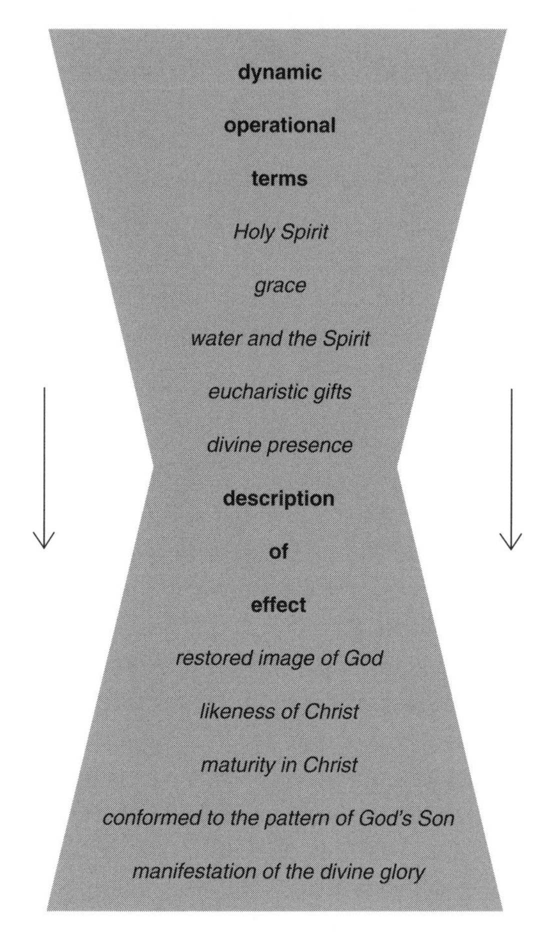

Figure 2 The cause and effect dynamics of formation

This interpretive grid is suggested by the wider linguistic structures and context in which formational language occurs in recent Church of England liturgical texts, and designates or presupposes the divine presence (both Word and Spirit) as being the agent of the transformation of the worshippers themselves. The difficulty here, of course, is that like accounting for "answers to prayer," the intended change in the worshipper is notoriously difficult to predict or adequately describe in generalized terms.

The analysis leaves us with two questions. First, why has formational language become prevalent? And, second, so what?

So *why* has "formational vocabulary" become so prevalent in the official Church of England's liturgical revision? A number of related questions suggest themselves. Is its repeated occurrence merely a rhetorical strategy to ensure that participants might get the point of worship? Or, and perhaps more cynically, is it a curious exercise in self-persuasion about something that is becoming more difficult to believe in? Is the ever-increasing production of new liturgical texts a frantic attempt to counter the growing weakness of religious discourse and the collapse of a public rhetoric in Western culture? If it is solely this, then it will be ultimately self-defeating. Is it that our religious discourse has become so weak that we have to spell it out continuously and hammer it home? Is it that in our day we need to make explicit in our worship texts those messages that were received implicitly in previous generations? But, as George Steiner (1991) argues, language can still echo with a largely forgotten meaning and resonate with our experience; so perhaps the prevalence of formation vocabulary in contemporary liturgical writing is the catching of such an echo and the making explicit of a recovered conviction that worship can be the theatre of human transformation. Such a recovered appreciation (if not conscious conviction) is suggested by the analysis of the vocabulary and by the direct correlation we have plotted between the multifarious expressions of our being shaped into the Body of Christ and the references to and invocations of the dynamic Spirit of God.

Pursuing the question "Why?" leads us to retrieve a forgotten aim of liturgical renewal, which moved the twentieth–century Liturgical Movement. It is ironical that this recovery coincided with the feverish pace of liturgical revision that one could understandably take to have been the goal of liturgical renewal. But liturgical revision was by no means the only, or necessarily primary, task of liturgical renewal. Its true goal was the fruition of Christian life, but this was overtaken and somewhat occluded by the clamor for new worship texts and the debates over accessibility and the language in which our worship is cast.

Christians are called to worship in Spirit and in truth. But that Spirit needs to be discerned, and perhaps some of what we might attribute to the Spirit is actually a manifestation of the spirit of the age. One of the dangers of movements for religious renewal is that they sail close to the spirit of the age. It might be, for example, that what we take to be the stirring of God's Spirit is actually a manifestation of the impulse for and need to claim individual and immediate experience of God in those living in a highly individualized culture that offers instant gratification and entertainment. As the apostle Paul insisted, we need to discern the Spirit, and that Spirit is given for "the common good" (1 Corinthians 12:7); its gifts and graces are given for the building up of the corporate Body, the Church (Ephesians 4:12). The Spirit is given, in other words, to enhance the corporate identity of the worshipping community and not to induce inner religious feelings or experience in individual worshippers. As we learn from the story of the sending of the Spirit at Pentecost, the Spirit of God is sent to undo the curse of Babel and unite a disparate group of people. The unity given and made by the Spirit does not override our diversity, however, for it was distributed severally upon each of those gathered in the upper room, and each heard the apostles' teaching in their *own* language. Each receives the gift that they may be one, and so the Spirit orchestrates the prayer of a worshipping community, enabling a diverse assembly of people to pray with one heart and voice in the first person plural: "*Our* Father . . . ."

We are called to worship both in Spirit and in truth, and true worship will provide the conditions in which the fruits of the Spirit (Galatians 5:22, 23) might come to maturity in the lives of Christians. Worship in Spirit and in truth leads, in other words, to the making of the Christian within the common life and worship of the Body of Christ, the Church, and it is precisely this that has become the largely forgotten, but original primary aim, of liturgical renewal.

The aim of worship as the forming of Christians is enshrined in the documents of renewal. As has already been noted, the most influential document for the Western Church was the *Sacrosanctum Concilium* document of Vatican II. Section 11 of this document dealt with issues of liturgical formation, with the need of worshippers to become more aware of what they do when they engage in worship; but the following and less frequently quoted Section 12 of the document addressed the question of the formation of the Christian within the corporate body of worshippers. At the center of liturgical reform was the forming of the Christian; its immediate aim was the forming of the worshipper, changing the person, for which changing the form of worship was but the means. The goal of forming the worshipper accords with the *lex orandi*, the law of prayer, enshrined in the form of the rite itself.

At the heart of the eucharistic offering in the Western Roman rite is the prayer that the Lord "may fashion us for himself." The term "fashion," a key term in the intentional language of the rite, indicates what Edward Kilmartin (1998, 355) called the ultimate meaning of the eucharistic celebration, namely, the shaping of those who participate in it. This focus on the formation of the worshipper concurs with the Eastern Orthodox view of liturgical renewal articulated by the influential writer Fr. Alexander Schmemann. He consistently argued that the primary goal of liturgical reform was the shaping of the Christian as a member of Christ's Body, the Church. The Eucharist, he said, was the sacrament of the Church and transformed us again and again into *membra Christi* (see Fisch, 1990, p. 114). As is often remarked, the Church makes the Eucharist and the Eucharist makes the Church. But interestingly it was the Anglican monk of Nashdom, Dom Gregory Dix, who in *The Shape of the Liturgy* (1945) drew attention to how the Church was made by making Eucharist long before it was fashionable to cite Orthodox and Roman writers on this topic. In the Methodist tradition, this view of the Eucharist making the Church is at least implicit in John Wesley's understanding of the Communion as being a "converting ordinance." Thus we can argue that across the denominational spectrum there is an extraordinarily wide ecumenical convergence on the conviction that the Eucharist has a profound formative effect in the shaping of worshippers into a real Christlikeness.

The corollary of this effect of the celebration of the Eucharist is that worshippers themselves need to be open to being configured to the paschal mystery of Christ's death and resurrection, and to pray as that mystery is celebrated in the Eucharist that Christ might "fashion us for himself." For the very point and purpose of worship is that the worshipper might be shaped by the pattern of Christ's death and resurrection. So the answer to the question as to why formational language is so prevalent in our worship texts is that it brings to expression and makes explicit the most profound purpose of worship—the fashioning of the Christian in conformity to Christ.

The question of why we worship could simply be put in terms of why we go to church. There might be many valid answers to this, but the basic fact is that we are called, invited by Christ to be his companion and to be drawn into community one with another. As George Herbert understood so well, God's grace can override our feelings of disconnectedness and resist our instinct to draw back from love's invitation: "Love bade me welcome . . . and I did sit and eat" ("Love III"). We go to church because we are invited, and as someone so perceptively said, we should go not for what we might get out of it, but because of what we might bring to it. Worshippers might well require some liturgical re-education to grasp fully this point as it does run counter to the kind of assumptions and motives that are so deeply ingrained in us. So, what do we bring when we gather with others for worship? At one level, what we might bring to worship is simply ourselves; we literally present ourselves, and should make ourselves truly present to both the call and gentle working of God's grace. Second, and of equal importance, we bring all the cares and concerns that press upon us, the people we love, and those entrusted to our care into the arena of God's healing mercy and transforming grace as the drama of salvation unfolds before us in the words, symbols and sacramental signs of worship.

Salvation, of course, is a complex theological word, a technical term in the religious word box, and one that has a range of different connotations. An amusing story is told at Mirfield of a member of the Community of the Resurrection, Fr. Geoffrey Beaumont, being approached by an earnest evangelical as he relaxed on a deckchair while on holiday at the seaside. When asked if he had been saved, he replied rather curtly, but not without a hint of mischievous amusement, "No, I haven't even been in yet!" Salvation can well be seen as being rescued from danger, as a lifeguard might save a person caught in the flow of a turning tide. But note, it is a question of being saved *from* something. What we need to be saved from can be something quite individual—perhaps something about our past—but it can also be more general—the need to be saved from some calamity—or the consequences of a corporate sin—racism, or a sad and violent episode in the history of a people or nation, for example. In religious terms we frequently speak of being saved *from* sin and its deadly consequences, and again, this is invariably some past action of which we are ashamed, or a past failure that paralyzes us in the present. But we are not only saved from things such as danger or disaster, but also saved *for* something. The gift of salvation in the present not only looks back, but also looks forward. It is not only to do with the *past,* but also with the *future,* of what might come to be. Seeing the future as well as the past referred to in the word and work of salvation is crucial, and again can furnish us with an answer to the question of why we go to church and engage in worship. Yes, we are certainly saved from something, but for what and to what end? The answer is that we are not only saved from the past, we are also being saved for a particular purpose, namely the working out of God's design for us and those for whom we pray.

The end of worship, we might say, is our transformation into the likeness of Christ; that quite simply is the end or point of worship, of our being invited, addressed and fed by the risen Christ in the power of the Spirit. We gather for worship and open ourselves (open, that is, our whole selves, all that makes us the person we are) to the imperceptible working out of the divine purposes. In one sense, we are what we become, but what we might become is what we allow God to make of us. And what does God want to make of us? In one of his sermons St. Augustine answers in rather stark and surprising terms: "God wishes to make you god" (Sermon 166.4). Taking this as our cue, we could say that we go to church and gather for worship because God seeks to make us gods (an expression from Psalm 82:6, "you are gods," and placed on the lips of Jesus in John 10:34). What this means is that we are adopted as God's children by grace, through being joined to Christ in baptism. What sustains us in being and seeking to live as the children of God is our sharing in the being and life of Christ in Communion (see 1 Corinthians 10:16), and through the indwelling transfiguring grace of the Holy Spirit. Finally, we can see that when we speak of being saved, we speak of being saved from something and of being saved for something, but the implication of this is that we are being saved *into* something, saved from lives disfigured by sin, into lives transfigured by grace. This final meaning certainly accords with Paul's exhortation that we are to "glorify God in our body" (1 Corinthians 6:20b).

This theological excursion does shed light on the place of formational language in worship, but there are other factors that might also account for its prevalence and popularity. Just why has it become such a major theme in contemporary liturgical rhetoric? Perhaps we might detect here a trace of contemporary culture and of social trends. One can certainly see how talk of a person being changed might appeal to a culture obsessed with images of the self, of how we look and equally how we are seen by others and ranked on the social scale; likewise, talk of the formation of the self would also resonate in a society in which the individual is driven by the imperative to "make something of oneself." These observations are valid and pertinent and focus for us again that most pressing question of how we construe the relationship between Christianity and culture, and of how we might locate ourselves on the social map of postmodern life. The language of formation, of the worshipper being shaped by Christ, undoubtedly resonates with the modern obsession with the self, and the compulsion to keep fit and to look good. Increased social mobility and financial means expand opportunities to change location and employment, and what a person does and where they live provide the index for constructing and deciphering personal identity. We define ourselves not only in terms of occupation, but also in terms of our purchasing power: "I buy, therefore I am" and what I buy makes me who I am. Indeed, there is a whole market offering personal "make-overs," opportunities to reinvent ourselves, as though the "self" was a commodity we could buy. Such a construct as the "self" is a chimera, momentarily caught in the hauteur of the fashion model, who in seeking to become an icon of beauty, ironically disdains the physicality of his or her actual physical body and etiolates the "self." Too often, it seems, we seek to cut a figure, make an impact, but dislike ourselves because of what we are and the way we look. Modern life, driven by the engine of global consumerism, is like living in a hall of mirrors. We live in a media-saturated society, and are constantly bombarded by advertisements projecting images of svelte young bodies. No wonder that when we catch a reflection of ourselves, our immediate thought is: "How do I look?" But this question is a question of appearance, and not the deeper question of our identity: "Who am I?"

Identity itself is a modern word and is at best a rather nebulous concept. In a society in which the therapeutic domain is seen as the source of personal well-being, it is not surprising that a culture of "self-realization" and "self-improvement" has become all-pervasive. But the aggressive pursuit of these personal aims and aspirations can result in the dissipation of the self, and our attempt to recover a sense of who we are can further entrench the "self." Let me indicate what I mean by the dissipation of the self. The self is dissipated on those occasions when we find ourselves on the edge, when the claims made on us have been so great that we feel "wrung out," and there is little of us left to give. This is an all too familiar scenario in a work-dominated culture, where the deals I can strike bring recognition as well as financial gain, and so become the index of "who I am." The pressing imperative for the contemporary individual is to "network"; the working of contacts is evidently the means of gaining personal advantage, and such networking is invariably compelled by the demands of work and the workplace. But this is at considerable relational and personal cost: the danger is that networking encroaches on and displaces deeper relationships of personal intimacy and friendship.

This leads us to the second and related question of the entrenching of the self in the self. The sheer pace and relentless pressure of contemporary life can all too easily drive the individual to the dizzying edge of the self, to that psychological precipice where the individual can barely hold on to a sense of who they are. Driven to such limits the fortunate individual is helped to recover the self, perhaps through psychotherapy, through which they might regain a degree of self-possession. The expression "self-possession" is telling and exposes the limits of psychotherapy. Charles Taylor in his major book *Sources of the Self* (1989) tells how our individual sense of who we are comes to expression and is formed when we tell another "who we are." One can see how a narrative, a telling of our story, can give both a sense of coherence and direction to the episodic character of modern mobile life. But the limits of psychotherapy are imposed by its very procedure; the telling of the story is essentially self-referential, and the process of retrieval and its rehearsal might well result in a greater entrenchment of the self in the self. For in the recital of the self, the telling of one's story, the self reinforces itself, and the circle is closed within a self-referential cycle of subjectivity. The positive outcome might well be a greater sense of self-confidence and self-esteem, but the attendant, though not inevitable, danger is a greater solidification and guarding of the self. The guarded self is wary of meeting others and will only meet the world on its own terms. Really to engage with others and be open to the world would be too risky for the delicate equilibrium of the reconstructed self.

Undoubtedly the image of the modern self I have sketched is that of a caricature, but as with every cartoon it depicts the salient features of its subject by way of exaggeration. In this instance, the cartoon is of a Humpty Dumpty figure that, having to bear the sheer weight of the significance which we ascribe to the "self," is in the final analysis unstable. No wonder, then, that we find ourselves enmeshed in an all-pervasive culture of self-help and almost narcissistic self-regard. Within such a cultural matrix, the Christian quest characterized in the gospel by "losing oneself to find oneself" appears incomprehensible. The challenge this presents is to find a way through the clash of cultures. But how far can we extricate ourselves from the conditions of modernity that insidiously shape our attitudes in ways of which we are barely aware? We are all culturally conditioned, and the culture we question is the one in which we are embedded. This egocentric culture, marked by a strident individualism and its prized goal of personal autonomy (literally meaning "a law to *oneself!*") is inimical to corporate Christian worship and corrosive of its concomitant living of the common life. Two options as to where Christians individually, and the Church institutionally, might situate themselves on this map of modernity immediately come to mind. The first, entertained by ultra-conservative groups, both Catholic and Evangelical, is a retreat into an essentially private religious world. But such a route is precluded by the fact that it is precisely *this* world that is called into God's reign of justice and peace. The second option, typically espoused by liberals, is that of a deliberate accommodation of modernity. But again such a capitulation to the contemporary cultural norms and social trends is precluded by the fact that God's Kingdom is *not* of this world.

A thorough and insightful analysis of these quandaries is given by Graham Hughes in his *Worship as Meaning* (2003), and although the detailed analysis helps to clear the ground, his positive strategic proposal of how we might signify "God" under the conditions of late modernity is not finally satisfying theologically. What is needed is something more radically orthodox, radical in its critical engagement with contemporary culture, and orthodox in the primary connotation of the word *doxology* (that is, worship), and in being more deeply rooted in, and in speaking from, an inhabited tradition of Christian thought and truth.

In his book, Hughes takes up the concept of "limit experiences" from the semiotic theory of the American philosopher C. S. Pierce. Hughes presents these limit experiences as those occasions when the familiar world is intensified, and works with the useful notion of "the boundary," a kind of virtual frontier of human existence that he maps as the locus of our human encounter with the holy. What he says in describing these limit experiences, those occasions when we find ourselves on the edge, as he says, of the platform of life, is extraordinarily insightful. Appropriating the category of limit experiences, Hughes illustrates what he means by being on the edge of existence in describing those moments of ecstatic elation and near despair, occasioned by shock, or surprise, an achievement or accident, and in which we both advertently and inadvertently find ourselves from time to time. But in charting these limit experiences and in tracing the edge of human existence, Hughes stops short of that frontier which is the *liminal* threshold, as named in the anthropologist von Gennep's analysis of a rite of passage. The liminal threshold designates an "in-between space" in which the self is realigned and changed, and although Hughes uses the word "liminal," he does not actually apply this interpretative model of liminality to show the meaning of worship. So let me briefly indicate how this model might be applied to "limit experience," and how it might throw light on those occasions when we commemorate the paschal mystery of Christ's death and resurrection in the celebrations of baptism and the Eucharist.

The ultimate limit according to the Christian story was reached in the calamitous death of the Son of God, who was crucified "outside of the city" beyond the designated bounds, that is, of a civilized and just political domain. In the Gospel accounts of the crucifixion, the final limit is heralded by the cry of dereliction: "My God, my God, why have you forsaken me?" Paradoxically, though, this total dispossession of self by Christ was also an act of conferral and self-gift; hence the other words from the cross in Luke's narrative: "Into your hands I commend my spirit." The cross, in marking as it does the final edge of divine abandonment and total gift, becomes the boundary at which others meet and are drawn into relationship with each other. At the place of the cross, the frontier between God and the abyss of nothingness, relationships are reconfigured according to that closest human bond, the bond between a mother and her child: "Woman, behold your son" and "Son, behold your mother." In the classical tradition of Christian iconography and reflection, the cross represents the source of the gospel sacraments of baptism and Eucharist: for out of the crucified flowed both water and blood, so that the place where baptism and Eucharist are celebrated becomes the site of the cross. The meaning is extended, and the place of baptism and the place of Communion become *liminal* places, frontiers at which identity is conferred and relationships are reconfigured to the image and likeness of Christ. In worship we approach the mysterious Other who is God, drawn by the Spirit and claimed by Christ, and in that encounter the Christian receives his or her true self as a gift donated by God's gratuitous grace. As the Christian approaches the boundary of that liminal space, symbolized by the designated space of baptism, and the place where Communion is received, the self is decentered in the response of faith and in the assent of the "Amen" (so be it!). And some might come to say with Paul: "that which I formally held dear I now regard as refuse" (Philippians 3:7), for "it is no longer I who live, but Christ who lives in me" (Galatians 2:20b). For in the sacramental encounter and exchange, the "ego," in other words, is thrown from the center of our universe, as we share in a greater life and being, that of the One who died and who now lives, the One through whom all things are reconciled and in whom all things find their final coherence ("hold together" Colossians 1:17), identity and fulfillment (Ephesians 1:10). Worship, we might say, is the school where the individual ego learns what it is to be a person, in communion with God and in community with others. Such a view is supported by Alistair McFadyen's recent attempt to construct a systematic theology of personhood in social and relational terms. McFadyen (1990, p. 31) concludes that the individual Christian person "images God" most fully as a worshipping self: that is, when the person joins with others in "returning" to God in a movement of thanks and praise." So we could say that in worship we come to ourselves and indeed receive our true identity in the transformation of the self. But such a claim is couched in rather abstract terms. How might we begin to elucidate its meaning in terms of our actual participation in worship? In answering this question we shall first register the key theological point of reference and then draw on the philosophical work of Paul Ricoeur to help us see how the language we use for our worship might actually work.

First and theologically, to elucidate the formational meaning of worship we need to work with a more developed pneumatology (a theology of the Holy Spirit) and accordingly give a greater logical priority to the presence and active working of God. Within such a framework, the assumed primary sense of the catch-phrase of the twentieth-century Liturgical Movement, "active participation," would need to be inverted, so that the accent was placed not so much on *our* active participation (i.e. what worshippers actually did, said and sang when they gathered for worship) but upon how it is the worshippers themselves who are, in a real sense, the ones who are acted upon; perhaps a more appropriate nomenclature might be something like "responsive participation." This is not, of course, a call for the disenfranchising or silencing of worshippers, but an appeal for us to see in this strange business of worship another perspective, one that was clearly alluded to by Michael Ramsey when he stated that when it came to experimenting with a new liturgical text, the question was not what we made of it, but what it might make of us.

If the emphasis is to be placed on the action of God in worship, as our analysis of the word-field demonstrates that it should, something needs to be said about the concomitant disposition and expectations of those who gather for worship. A liturgical text can only propose, and its embodied performance only set the mood and conditions for the appropriation of what is proposed. What is required is a particular disposition on the part of the worshipper. For the unfolding of the mystery of salvation through Christ and the Spirit in a liturgical celebration has to be met and received by the worshipper, who needs to be open to receive what is offered and given in the dynamic exchange of worship. This, as we have said, presupposes a particular disposition on the part of the worshipper. We might characterize it as an expectation and openness to the possibility of being changed in response to the divine presence, which is both invoked and expressed in the act of worship. We must come to worship, in other words, not only consciously, but attentively and with a more contemplative and receptive approach.

For many of us this entails a significant shift in attitude, and therefore presents a considerable challenge to how we conceive the meaning of worship. Further, a more contemplative approach to worship would require a tectonic shift in how we engage in liturgical education and in the ways in which we might actively enable and encourage the people of God, both lay and ordained, to enter more fully (and dare I say, more expectantly?) into the prayer of the Church. What is needed is not even more information about worship, but a greater sensibility to it, the kind of sensibility that can best grow by deliberately immersing oneself in the culture of a worshipping community. The analogy that immediately suggests itself is the learning of a foreign language, which as everyone says, is best learned by spending time actually living in the country. Liturgical formation also takes time and requires specific conditions, such as the regular practice of a prayer, which perhaps is not best served by the kind of "liturgical consumerism" that leads us to demand or provide new, challenging and surprising experiences in our worship. Of course the gospel must be expressed afresh in each generation, our worship inculturated (as it always has been), but this should be balanced by the recognition of how worship provides the *stabilitas* of a Christian community. Such stability is a necessary prerequisite for the ongoing practice of prayer that our formation in the likeness of Christ requires. As one commentator has recently put it: "worship is not the occasion for the *self*-expression of the worshipping community, but first and foremost God's work on us" (see Godfried Cardinal Danneels' "Liturgy Forty Years After the Second Vatican Council: High Point or Recession" in Pecklers, 2003, p. 9). Liturgy, in other words, is not the occasion for us to express what we are (a means of self-expression) but an invitation to us both to hear and to receive what we are yet fully to become through the call of the Word and the operation of the Spirit.

If worship is seen in this perspective of transformation, then one might say that the liturgy is the occasion *par excellence* for the unmasking (the act of confession?) and remaking of the *self* (in the ritual acts of baptism, sharing the peace, and preeminently in the act of Communion?). Through these repeated acts our liturgical formation is, as in the Benedictine understanding of the "conversion of life," a lifelong process. Again, like the visitor seeking to learn the language of a foreign country, we too need to immerse ourselves in the culture, in this case, the culture of the Church's prayer, allowing it to work on us and to go on allowing it to work on us until "Christ is formed in us." Further illumination is shed on all this as we reflect more on how the language of worship might actually work.

In seeking a theoretical elucidation of liturgical formation one might look for a liturgical hermeneutic that draws on the work of Paul Ricoeur. Ricoeur was interested in the texture, the function of language and how we might appropriate its meaning—the art of hermeneutics. His work has its limitations in that the focus of his reflections are on the nature of a text as *text,* a fixed body of writing existing independently of both the reader and the author. But the insights he draws are illuminating and, if not immediately transferable, can help us as we begin to elucidate how a liturgical text, when it is performed in the actual event of worship, might work for us. According to Ricoeur the reader's quest is not so much in seeking to get behind the text—say to the author's original intention in writing—but in seeing what the text opens up for the reader in terms of how they understand themselves and place themselves in the world. The text proposes a world, and our reading of a text is as much a work of the imagination as of comprehension. Thus the very act of reading, Ricoeur ventures to say, introduces us into the imaginative variations of the ego, of how we might see ourselves and relate to the world around us. Unsurprisingly, then, Ricoeur gives a privileged position to poetry and the work of fiction in opening up new worlds for us to inhabit and different ways of relating to others. In this sense, the aim of interpretation is not recovering a hidden meaning behind the text, but coming to see what Ricoeur describes as "the world in the text." So, in seeking to understand what a text is about, what Gadamer called "the matter of the text," the reader has to be open to the world, or our "being-in-the world" (*pace* Heidegger) which is "in front of the text." As we have seen, what the text offers is essentially an imaginative world, but can such a redescribed world have any reference to or bearing upon the everyday world? This question presses us against the limits of Ricoeur's method, but also points to his most illuminating idea, namely that the kind of world, or description of how we might be in our world proposed by the text, is unrealized and has to do with *potentiality* and not with simply stating how things actually are or how we feel. It is quite simply a question of opening new horizons, of seeing new possibilities and recognizing that the world we inhabit can be different, and that we ourselves can change.

The written text, through the conceits of narrative, parable and metaphor, presents a new world for the reader to inhabit. Ricoeur (1981: 142) expresses this in these terms:

> new possibilities of being-in-the-world are opened up within everyday reality. Fiction and poetry intend being, not under the modality of being-given, but under the modality of power-to-be. Everyday reality is thereby metamorphised by what could be called the imaginative variations which literature carries out on the real.

What is taken to be "the real world" is taken up and redescribed in the writing of literature, and that imaginary world can only be entered by the reader. Ricoeur insists on the necessity of the reader being open to the text: "exposing ourselves to the text and receiving from it an "enlarged self ". In one sense the text does promise and hold open new ways of "being-in-the-world," but the appropriation of "the world of the text," allowing the meaning of the text to enter you, leads to the transformation of the reader. This, Ricoeur says (1981: 158), is the goal and culmination of the hermeneutical process: "the self-interpretation of the subject who henceforth understands himself better, understands himself differently, or simply begins to understands himself." C. S. Lewis once said that the reason we read is that we need to discover that we are not alone in the universe; reading can extend horizons and helps us to connect with and relate to others. Ricoeur takes this even further and says that we read or perform a text (including a musical score or a religious rite) in order to be *changed,* to discover and make our own new and different ways of being in the world and relating to others. It is, of course, through the actual practice of these ways of being and relating that the everyday tangible world itself can be, and comes to be, transformed.

These philosophical reflections recall the poet Anne Stevenson's suggestive line: "the way you say the world is what you get," recalling for us the poetic power of disclosure, of showing the extraordinary in the ordinary which we explored earlier in Chapter 3.

These reflections on the texts and readings can extend analogously to liturgical texts, and taking our cue from Ricoeur we could say that liturgical texts propose new self-understandings, new bases for relating to others, and new points to orient ourselves, to give direction to our life. Again, one might draw a parallel between how, in Ricoeur's terms, a reader approaches a text and how a worshipper might take his or her place and participate in worship, for both require an open and receptive approach. The performance of a text, likened by Gadamer and Ricoeur to the phenomenon of play, can be transformative for the participant, and so those who would perform liturgical texts should recognize that they are liable to be changed by the event of worship. After all, worship is a way of "playing heaven on earth," and there is no more serious play than what that prophetic voice of the twentieth-century Liturgical Movement, Romano Guardini, described as "the wondrous playfulness of liturgy."

But there is a final point to draw from our philosophical foray that is anchored in Ricoeur's understanding of how the reader apprehends the proposed world of a text. There is not only "the reception of an enlarged self" but also "the relinquishment of the self" (1981, pp. 182, 183). For every act of appropriation has its counterpart in disappropriation; put more colloquially, every gain has its loss and can expose the distance between who we are and what we might be. When we come to possess a new self there has to be a kind of dispossession, as every act of loving another entails a letting go. To transpose this to a liturgical frame of reference, to the realm of the "worshipping self," we might speak in terms of a "remaking" (for example, in the liturgical act of Communion) in order that the individual ego might be reconfigured to the form of Christ, and its counterpart, the "unmaking" (for example, in the liturgical act of confession). In Ricoeur's terms the final goal of hermeneutics is the giving of "*self* to the *ego*"; for us this is only possible when those who participate in worship are open and responsive to the transformative operation of God's creative and renewing Spirit. In the end, then, we might say that real liturgical work is not so much the shaping of worship as the shaping of the worshipper, within the Body of the Church, into the likeness of Christ, for "Christ has no body now on earth, but ours" (attributed to St. Teresa of Avila). How our embodied selves might become and be understood as being Christ's Body is a question that we will explore and seek to explicate further in our treatment of the celebrations of baptism and Eucharist in the following two chapters.

5
Transforming Rites

In the previous chapter we tracked the use of the language of formation in liturgical revision and noted its increased frequency in recent authorized liturgical texts and seasonal resources. I attempted to evaluate critically the incidence of this language and offered some suggestions as to why it has become so prevalent and how we might understand the function of these texts in bearing the promise of a different way of being in the world. We now turn our attention from the content of liturgical texts to the form of liturgy, to see how the texts work by being performed in the interplay of sight, sound and bodily movement that constitutes an act of liturgical celebration. To illustrate the vital connection between the content and form of liturgy we might take our cue from Ricoeur and say that what is proposed in the liturgical text (the reconfiguring of ourselves to the form of Christ) is in some sense performed in the event of sacramental celebration. The rites, we might say, are *enacted* and are enacted bodily. But first we must establish why the body plays such a central role in the Christian drama of salvation, and take up again its foundation story.

The story of Jesus entering and cleansing the temple in the holy city of Jerusalem is placed at the beginning of John's Gospel, suggesting that the incident itself holds the key to understanding the person and saving work of Christ (John 2:13–25). The temple was the "holy place" and its complex of buildings included the Holy of Holies, the sacred site where God's glory dwelt, and where only the high priest entered, and that only on one occasion in the year, the Feast of Yom Kippur, the Day of Atonement. In her recent published studies, Margaret Barker (2003) has drawn attention to the symbolic setting of the temple ritual, and argued that the atonement was understood not only as the occasion when the sins of God's people were "wiped away," but also as the healing, restoration and renewal of creation itself. The temple complex of buildings was divided into clearly delineated spaces, in which the people of God could stake their claim in the odoriferous commerce between heaven and earth played out in the complex system of temple sacrifices. But when Jesus entered the temple he overturned the tables of the money-changers and the sellers of pigeons, and thereby demonstrated that he was the one who would attain salvation for God's people. It was a prophetic and priestly action that signaled the inauguration of a new era, a new deal in the divine-human exchange, and a radical revaluation of the economy of salvation. The *commercium* between humanity and God was no longer to be transacted with the flesh of birds and animals, but in and through a human body (see Hebrews 9:12). For in entering the temple, the place of sacrifice, Christ presages his impending self-offering and declares that his body will be the new sanctuary, the arena where humanity might encounter and be changed by God's holiness. This sacred site came to be clearly identified by the writer of the Letter to the Hebrews: "we have been sanctified through the offering of the body of Jesus Christ once for all" (Hebrews 10:10), and in his person, his "body of flesh" presaged that sacrifice which would secure our human redemption and reconciliation to God and with each other (see Colossians 1:22).

The prophetic "cleansing of the temple" demonstrated that the true site of exchange between God and humanity was the place of prayer, for God had declared: "My house shall be called a house of prayer"; the promised salvation would be transacted and cashed out not over the table of the money-changers but *bodily,* in and through the bodily fate of Christ himself. Christ's very bodily appearing represented the minting of a new currency, a new means of value and exchange between God and humanity. In John's account of this incident, the religious authorities are outraged by the claim Jesus made by entering the temple, but the irony is that they themselves were complicit and unwittingly instrumental in changing the currency of divine-human exchange in the economy of salvation. For it was they who brought him bound to Caiaphas, the high priest, and who alleged that Christ had said: "In three days I will destroy this temple, and raise it up in three days." At this point in the narrative, the evangelist adds the explanatory note for his readers, that in speaking of the temple, Jesus referred to his *body.* Christ, in other words, embodied a new temple; in his own person, the divine and human were conjoined and made one. And to prove the full extent of Christ's human nature, and to disclose the divine purpose, his body was destined to suffer, to die and to be laid in the tomb until the third day when he would be vindicated by God and gloriously raised from the dead in the power of the Spirit. For ultimately, the embodied Word could not be silenced. The divine love could not be sealed up, shut up in a cold tomb, but had to have free movement towards and between others, that he might draw them also to the Father. So it happened that after the dawn of Easter, Christ moved among them and allowed himself to be seen by Peter, and by various combinations of the disciples, both in Jerusalem and on the shore of the Sea of Tiberias. And through these individual encounters the risen Lord prefigured how innumerable bodies would be called and reconfigured at one, uniting body of the crucified and risen Christ. The Church was to become his risen Body in and for the world.

As we read the post-resurrection appearances of Christ, we see how the encounters between the risen Christ and the disciples were occasions when relationships were reconfigured to the new resurrection Body of Christ. The apostle Thomas, far from being "doubting," was honest and insistently realistic in his response to the risen Christ. If what God had done was to be of any earthly use, then it had to have occurred in the domain of the body, in the reality that his and that of every human being. But the story of encounter with the risen Christ that has had the greatest impact upon the Christian imagination is the poignant meeting between Mary Magdalene and the risen Christ. It has inspired some of the finest Christian art, and Rilke's poem on the subject ("The Risen One"), must surely rank as one of the most sublime treatments of the themes of love and transcendence. In the Gospel story, the gentle rebuke of Christ to Mary Magdalene, "Touch me not," was a declaration that the body of the risen Christ, though still marked with the scars of human suffering, was not a body to be grasped or possessively held by any one individual. For in the reality of the resurrection, Christ's embrace is open for everybody and is universal in its scope. So Mary Magdalene had to learn that the body of Jesus could no longer be held, because that body had, as it were, to hold every-body. She might reach out to Jesus in her desire, but had yet to realize that she was already firmly held in Christ's undying and constant love. No longer were there to be private passions, for from the miraculous moment of resurrection an increasing number would be called and incorporated in that single expansive Body of Christ, that body which is the new temple.

This is how the first Christians began to make sense of the incomparable happening of the first Easter, and the metaphor of "bodily temple" was forged to depict the new reality. The physical body of each Christian was designated a "temple of the Holy Spirit" (1 Corinthians 6:19). The corporeal reference demanded a corporate frame of understanding, and so Paul tells the church at Corinth that they together were God's temple (1 Corinthians 3:16–17; cf. 2 Corinthians 6:16–18). The newly baptized were to be "built up, like living stones, into a spiritual temple" (1 Peter 2:5), a temple with the apostles as foundations and Christ Jesus himself as the chief cornerstone (Ephesians 2:20–22).

Through his suffering and death, the physical body of Jesus Christ became the site of total self-giving, the domain of inexhaustible divine blessings in the outflowing of water and blood from his body on the cross. Alongside Christ's sacrifice all other sacrifices appeared as being counterfeit currency in humanity's commerce with God, and according to the writer of the Epistle to the Hebrews, Christ was the new high priest, pioneering a new and living access into the presence of God, whose appearing transposed the worship of the temple and rendered it obsolete. The sacrificial commerce of the temple in Jerusalem had been superseded by Christ's body on the cross. Indeed, the very appearance of Christ presages a bodily sacrifice—"a body you prepare for me. . . . Lo, I come to do your will" (Hebrews 10:5)—that single and "sufficient sacrifice which effected our salvation, securing our peace with God, through his body on the cross" (Ephesians 2:14–16; cf. 1 Peter 2:24a). The indisputable message of the Epistle to the Hebrews is that the new Covenant, the new ordering of relationships between God and humanity, had been contracted through a body (the physical body of Jesus) and was presently inscribed by the Spirit on the hearts of those whose bodies were refreshed through the cleansing waters of Christian baptism.

What all this is saying is that our becoming Christian is essentially a kind of "body work," something that is worked out bodily. As we have seen, the "body" has become a major topic in current social theory and critical cultural commentary. In his three-volume work on the history of sexuality, the French philosopher Michel Foucault argues that the sexual body is shaped as much by cultural mores and conventions as by innate drives and physiological make-up. His analysis demonstrates how the "self" is negotiated in relationships of power and is continuously constrained and defined by social control and regulation. Foucault writes illuminatingly about the cultivation and practice of the self, but that "self" is regarded as a cultural construct and differs from one historical era and social setting to another. How far one might sustain the argument that the self is a cultural artifact is a debatable point, but we might play with the terms of Foucault's argument and say that the body of a Christian is the construct of the cultus, shaped in the liturgical setting and through the whole panoply and multifarious activity of Christian worship and sacramental celebration.

The idea that the making and shaping of Christians is a "body work" has distinct echoes in some of the earliest Christian writing, and was superbly caught and spelled out most emphatically by the second-century North African writer Tertullian. In a passage of his treatise on the resurrection of the body, Tertullian wrote:

> the flesh is the hinge of salvation . . . the flesh is washed in order that the soul may be cleansed; the flesh is anointed in order that the soul may be consecrated; the flesh is signed [with the cross] in order that the soul may be fortified; the flesh is overshadowed by the imposition of the hand in order that the soul may be illumined by the Spirit. The body feeds on the body and blood of Christ so that the soul might feast upon God (On the Resurrection of the Body 8:6–12).

The logical conclusion of Tertullian's argument against those who believed only in the immortality of the soul is that it is the whole indivisible person, body and soul, who is raised at the final resurrection of the dead, and this is precisely because the salvation offered and brought by Christ is played out on the actual physical body of the believer. What Tertullian suggests in this passage is that the story of salvation is inscribed on the flesh of the believer, and thereby becomes corporeal. This is evidenced in the fact that the individual points rehearsed by Tertullian in this cumulative argument, specify a particular liturgical ritual action, namely, the baptismal washing, the physical laying on of hands, the anointing with holy oil, and the receiving of the elements of Communion. In a similar vein, but in a later time and different location, Theodore of Mopsuestia (c. 350–428) repeatedly spoke of the reshaping of our nature in the homilies he delivered to the newly baptized.

The witness of these early Christian writers supports the view that the economy of salvation is cashed out bodily, and that what Christ offers and gives to humanity is effected through sacramental actions, using the elements of bread, olive oil and water to convey a spiritual currency through the medium of the physical body. Quite simply, the salvation proclaimed in the gospel is assimilated bodily, we might even say ingested, in both the receiving of the Word (note the use of this metaphor in connection with the Word in Ezekiel 2:8; 30:1–3 and Revelation 10:9–10) and the physical sacramental eating and drinking of Communion. It is precisely because salvation is physically transacted through the body that the very idea of a "virtual" Christian church through the Internet is an oxymoron.

Of course, thoughts and words, mental dispositions and emotional feelings, have a crucial part to play in our prayer and spiritual lives, but the element of ritual, of embodied action comes to prominence when we come to "glorify God in our body" (1 Corinthians 6:20b; cf. Philippians 1:20, where Paul speaks of Christ being honored in his body). It is significant that the vocabulary Paul uses here belongs to the language of worship, although admittedly in this context it opens out to refer to the actual living out of the Christian life. Nevertheless, the Christian life is grounded in worship, and springs from worship as its origin and source. Significantly, the incidence of Paul's "body language" again points to the fact that corporate Christian worship is essentially an embodied activity, and one that is enacted among and alongside the other bodies of those who have gathered for worship. A number of important practical consequences for how we conduct worship, and indeed how we might conduct ourselves in an act of worship, follows from this bodily perspective.

First, it highlights the importance of bodily posture in prayer, and alerts us to how our body language and the way we deport ourselves during an act of worship express what we are doing and the value of what we think it is about. It can, of course, work both ways: our body language can make the intended meaning of a liturgical moment more explicit and visible, and it can just as easily mask, distract or even contradict the meaning and mood of what happens in a given phase of a liturgical celebration. Take, for instance, the case of the president who sits back and crosses his or her legs for the Scripture readings, a clear body-language statement, if ever there was one, saying: "this is not an important element in the service!" In the Byzantine liturgy each phase of the unfolding drama is announced by the deacon calling the assembly to attention with instructions, such as, "Stand," or "Let us attend"—a salutary reminder that we should all, whether liturgical ministers or members of the congregation, be attentive throughout the liturgical celebration, and that the ways in which we might be attentive, fully present to what is happening, are as much through our bodily posture as through the engagement of our minds and hearts and spirit. Practically speaking, the way in which we deport ourselves, how we stand, move, sit or kneel, is also a mode of liturgical participation, and for this reason it is vital that those who plan and lead worship should consider the posture that should be adopted for the different parts of the liturgy, when, for instance, we might stand, kneel or sit. Different postures will help to express the meaning and mood of the different sequential phases of the liturgy. Equal attention should also be given to the physical movement which might occur, such as the presenting of the bread and wine (which need not be covered by the singing of a hymn), and where we might place ourselves in the liturgical space. Again, liturgical symbols, such as candles and lights, bread, wine and water, oils, Bible and Gospel book, and incense, ought to be clearly visible, and sensitively and imaginatively placed and handled. Correspondingly, particular ritual actions, such as the binding of the bride and bridegroom's hands at a celebration of marriage; the hand raised over the coffin for the dismissal prayer "Go forth, O Christian soul . . ." at a funeral; or the making of the sign of the cross at the absolution or blessing, need to be carefully articulated in a deliberate and expressive gesture, and one that is in proportion to the scale and physical setting in which the liturgy is being celebrated. Each ritual action, bodily movement or gesture ought to be deliberate, unhurried, never fussy and always visible to the whole worshipping assembly. (There is a danger that the actions of the Eucharist, for instance, might go unnoticed by worshippers if their eyes are constantly fixed to a printed text of one kind or another.) Our participation in worship is not only in saying or singing something, but also in looking, listening, and in doing, and doing something together, as one body. This even applies, and perhaps applies especially, at those moments in the liturgy such as the Eucharistic Prayer when the worshippers themselves are not actually doing anything, but when something is being done, in this instance by the president, which should command the full attention of each member of the congregation.

There is now a general consensus across the ecumenical spectrum of liturgical and sacramental theologians that the sacraments should be regarded as "rites" whose meaning is grounded in, and should not be divorced from, their actual liturgical celebration (see, for example, the work of the American Lutheran, Gordon Lathrop (1993) and the Catholic philosopher, P. J. FitzPatrick (1993). The celebration of the liturgy, in other words, is both the context and the locus in which we might read the meaning of sacraments and see the part they play in the making of Christians. When we do view the sacraments in the context of liturgical celebration, then we see them less as "things" and more as "ritual actions." Furthermore, the ritual action referred to here is the action of the whole rite that, as I have indicated, is the action of the whole worshipping community and not only of the presiding minister.

The performance of the rite, whether of baptism or Eucharist, is an ecclesial act and therefore one in which the whole worshipping community should participate. The ways in which members of the worshipping community actively participate are various and include: the gathering together with others, the standing to greet and attend to the reading of the Gospel (in order to greet and receive the divine Word who becomes present in the assembly), the sharing of the Peace with those around one, the presentation of the gifts of bread and wine, the physical act of moving to receive Communion, the actual receiving of the elements, and the very act of eating and drinking. In all these, and in other ways too, the individual worshipper interacts with others who have gathered for worship, but most importantly, even in what appears to be an unconscious "going through the motions," the worshipper enacts and appropriates by embodying the various meanings of the different moments of the liturgical celebration. To put the matter simply, when it comes to the sacraments, we get the meaning of them by doing them, and because the "doing of the liturgy" is (or should be) such a bodily exercise, then the assimilation of the meaning is immediate and can become deeply ingrained in us precisely because it is embodied. As Theodore Jennings argues in a seminal article entitled "On Ritual Knowledge" (1982), we apprehend the reality of God's presence primarily in and through the body, and what we learn through ritual we learn through simply and repeatedly performing it. Rather as we come to learn the rules of a game by actively playing it, so the meaning of sacramental worship is gained by our practice, our participation in liturgical celebrations; and through what I have called this "body work," the meaning is appropriated through the sensual body, as much through the senses of touch and taste as in seeing and hearing. But at this juncture of the discussion we should recall the point registered in Chapter 4, that when considering our participation in the liturgy, we should recognize it as being secondary, and see that all the various actions and movements made by the worshipper in the performance of the liturgy are essentially responsive gestures. For the place of worship, its setting, is the sacred space where the Spirit is invoked, so our actions are responses to the divine presence. It is the Spirit, the modes of the divine presence, which summon us and provoke a response in us, rather like the way in which our feet automatically begin to tap when we hear a stirring tune: the music sounds and we begin to move. So, in terms of our participation in the performance of the liturgy, our celebration is like a dance as we move to the movements of our partner, in this case the Spirit and the modes of Christ's presence, in Word, community and sacramental signs. What the rite "means" is literally embodied as we act it out following the pattern of the shape of the liturgy.

It was Dom Gregory Dix who famously argued that the Eucharist was primarily an action. The command of the Lord according to Luke and Paul's account of the institution of the Eucharist was, "Do this in remembrance of me" (where, significantly, the verb poieite is in the plural). The celebration of the liturgy is essentially a doing, taking, blessing, giving and receiving. The essential character of liturgy as "action" is simply illustrated by the fact that the word "eucharist" originates from a doing word, the Greek verb eucharistein, literally meaning "to give thanks". The Eucharist is a repeated and complex ritual action and the Cambridge systematic theologian David Ford (1999, pp. 164–165) has wistfully mused on the formative effect of this repeated action, habituated in the life of the regular worshipper:

> The imperative "Do this!" includes the wisdom of habituation that is embodied in liturgical practices. Repetition after repetition of hearing scripture and its interpretation, of repentance, of intercession and petition, the kiss of peace, of communion, of praising and thanking, all within a

> dramatic pattern that slowly becomes second nature: who can tell in advance what sort of self is being shaped year after year as these practices are interwoven thoughtfully with all the rest of life?

Although the effect of our participation in the liturgy evades any precise description, and importantly is beyond our control, what we can say is that the Christian is undoubtedly shaped by the shape of the liturgy.

Building on this conviction that the celebration of the liturgy is essentially a formative action, I would like to assert this more forcibly, pursue it further, probe a little more and ask a deeper, perhaps more theological question: not concerning what we do, in our performance of the ritual, but what might be happening in the event of a particular sacramental celebration. This question leads us beyond what we enact ritually to reflect on what it is that we might be responding to in our liturgical celebrations, how God's grace might operate and to what effect.

The liturgy is literally acted out, expressed in words and actions, in formal and repeated gestures, such as the taking and breaking of bread, the pouring of water and physical human touch. In all the ritual acts performed in the celebration of the liturgy, it is as if the finger of God and the finger of Adam in Michelangelo's famous painting on the ceiling of the Sistine Chapel, in Rome, finally make contact. The tension of fingers reaching out towards each other, but not actually touching, is resolved and contact is made, even if only momentarily, like the flash of recognition of Christ in "the breaking of bread" experienced by the two disciples at Emmaus, as humankind feels the touch of the divine presence. When we gather to celebrate the liturgy we find ourselves in the place where we might, in the very performance of the rite, come to know such sacramental moments. The rite, which includes the physical declaiming of Scripture in the readings and hearing of the Word, is the medium (though admittedly not the only possible one) through which the words of Scripture and liturgical texts can be scripted on our hearts and minds and their meaning assimilated. But this emphasis on our "ritual knowing" through the actual performance of liturgical actions in obedience to the Lord's command "Do this . . . ." needs to be balanced with the recognition that in the very doing of liturgy more is happening than meets the eye; something, we might say, is going on beyond the senses, which is not of our doing. There is a clue to what this is at the end of the preparatory prayers before the enarxis in the Byzantine liturgy, when the deacon announces: "It is time for the Lord to act!"

Following our conviction that art can sometimes bring our understanding to light, we can take up Aidan Kavanagh's (1990) suggestion about "seeing liturgically" and begin to elucidate this idea by looking at some of the early fifth- and sixth-century ecclesiastical art and architecture of Ravenna in order to see the meaning of what happens when Christians gather to celebrate baptism and the Eucharist. The mosaics, as we will see, are sumptuous and suggestive of a whole kaleidoscope of meanings. My contention is that we are able to read what is happening in sacramental celebration by looking carefully at the architectural space and the decoration of Ravenna's surviving early Christian art. Historically, the ecclesiastical architecture of Ravenna follows the pattern seen elsewhere in other early centers of Christian culture, such as the ancient see of Milan; but the surviving art, although made in a time of transition and innovation in artistic technique, is revealing both in terms of form and material. The mosaics were made of tessarae, small cubes of richly colored stone, metal and glass, and were placed unevenly to catch and play with the flickering light. This optical effect results in a shimmering and literally illuminating effect on the participants of the ritual being enacted on the floor space. When one looks, for instance, at the so-called Orthodox Baptistery built by Bishop Neon, one can trace a close correlation between the architectural shape, artistic decoration and the meanings of the rite of baptism. Baptism was commonly known as "enlightenment," and the artistic scheme gave both form and meaning to what was ritually enacted as the candidate was plunged in the water of the octagonal font, itself a symbol of the eighth day which, following the sequence of Genesis 1, marks the day of resurrection thereby representing the site of God's work of recreation.

It has already been noted that the overall effect of the sacramental celebration in such a setting would have made quite a dramatic impact on the participants, but one might go further and argue that the meanings of what was "done for the candidates" was articulated and modeled in visual artistic form. This view is supported by the use of visual language of both Ambrose of Milan and Cyril of Jerusalem who, in their discourses addressed to neophytes and catechumens a century earlier,

The Baptism of Christ, Baptistery of Theodoric, Ravenna

pressed home the significance of the setting and urged their listeners to "perceive" what they had physically seen with their eyes.

Taking this as our cue, let us look at the mosaics of the baptistery built by the Arian gothic king, Theodoric, at the end of the fifth-century to see how what is shown visually mediates the meaning of what is enacted ritually in the water-washing and anointing(s) of baptism.

The cupola medallion in the center of the domed ceiling directly above the font (see p. 102) is a mosaic of the baptism of Jesus. The composition is of three figures: first, John the Baptist standing on a large stone with his hand resting on the head of Jesus, ready to plunge him down into the water; second, the mythical figure of Jordan (who at the crossing of the Ark was driven back! (Psalm 114:3b) now has his left hand raised in a gesture of acclamation, acknowledging the true divinity of the Christ; third, along the central axis stands the figure of Jesus, and alone of the three figures he is in a frontal pose, thereby inviting the direct gaze of the viewer. The whole composition constitutes an icon which, when viewed, operates as a kind of visual epiphany or disclosure of the divine. For when we look attentively at this complex image we can see that it represents a moment of epiphany or divine disclosure. Indeed, the exact moment of epiphany is frozen in the shimmering mosaic; the dove (representing the descent of the Holy Spirit) with an effulgence of divine light emanating from its beak, signaling the moment when the heavenly voice declared: "You are my Son, the beloved, in whom I am well pleased." The art historian Gertrud Schiller (1971: p. 133) draws attention to the startling iconic effect of the image in the cupola in her description of how the various artistic elements vibrantly combine and complement each other:

> It is not only the dove and the light which exemplify the Epiphany, but also, as had already been the case fifty or sixty years earlier in the Baptistery of the Orthodox—the artistic means of composition and the shimmering gold ground.

What is physically seen artistically is the form of Jesus at his baptism, but what is revealed in the enacted ritual of baptism is the divine in human form, the "human form divine." And in this setting, when the sacrament of baptism is actually celebrated, what is perceived can also be recognized; as in a flash of poetic recognition, the newly baptized, still dripping from the gracious baptismal bath, recognize themselves in what is seen, and what they see is what they themselves have become. For in the iconic showing of "the human form divine" in the figure of Jesus Christ, the baptized see themselves and come to recognize and receive their newly conferred identity. The identity between Christ and the baptized was vividly spelled out with rhetorical flourish by Theodore of Mopsuestia who in his address to the newly baptized in Mopsuestia said: "He gave us new birth in holy baptism and made us his own body, his own "flesh, his offspring" (Baptismal Homily V, from

Yarnold, 1994). The contemporary reader might be surprised by the physical vocabulary which, incidentally, persists in the text of the Armenian baptismal rite which speaks of the baptized becoming "very body and limb" of the holy Church. Such corporeal language serves to reinforce the notion of identity between Christ and the Christian. But, returning to the passage cited from Theodore, the important point to draw out is the implicit understanding that what the candidate undergoes in the rite of Christian baptism is not some kind of charade or mimicry, but the occasion when a new identity (that is, a sense of who and what we are) is effectively conferred. This new identity is neither extraneous to us nor is it simply the relinquishing of ourselves because, as the terms of Theodore's account make clear, what we become in baptism is made, as it were, from the stuff of who we are. As he says, Christ "made us" his own body, etc., and with this crucial caveat we can say that in recognizing their new identity, those who are baptized come to themselves and come to receive themselves as a "gift." Such a view of the Christian self-understanding is entirely consistent with the New Testament witness that through water and the Spirit our very human nature is renewed in baptism (see Colossians 3:9–11; Titus 3:5b). The point is thrown into clear relief when we compare the mythical figure of Narcissus with the newly baptized emerging from the baptismal pool: unlike Narcissus who was mesmerized by his own reflection in a pool of water, those who are baptized are shown who they are and receive their true selves in looking beyond themselves and in facing or, more precisely, by being themselves faced by, Jesus Christ.

If we take the point made by Schillebeeckx and frequently cited in discussions on the sacraments, that Jesus Christ is the "primary sacrament," then every repeated sacramental action will ultimately refer to Christ, and Christ will be seen as the definitive self-communication of God to us. But how does Christ disclose and bring God to expression? As the "form" of God, Christ reveals the true and living God, but as the One who "emptied himself and took the form of our human likeness" (Philippians 2:6, 7) that disclosure and self-communication of God both reveals, and conceals, it is both shown and hidden. Yet, what is revealed is sufficient to impress upon us Christ's very image, the content of true formation. In speaking in these terms we need to clarify that the word "formation" in its classical Greek sense refers in the first instance to a drawing out of what is good and beautiful in a person, and does not imply pressing that individual into some kind of cramping mold! To construe formation in terms of a mere conventionality, or social conformity, would be a superficial and misleading understanding. In the context of our being shaped as Christians in the sacramental acts of Christian initiation, our formation works through the unique individuality of each person, so that in the case of each individual, it is that particular person, with their distinctive traits and characteristics, in whom Christ is being formed. Of course, there will inevitably be aspects of a person's character and possibly habits of behavior which will contradict the character of Christian life, and that is precisely why the process of being made Christian involves elements of repentance and renunciation. Indeed, the elements of repentance and renunciation were an equally dramatic act in the baptismal liturgy, ritually enacted in a turning away from sin and a turning towards Christ prior to the baptismal water-washing. This ritual of "turning away" was sometimes enacted by facing west, while the "turning towards" was literally a turning to face the east, which, is not only the direction of "Paradise," but also the horizon over which the new dawn breaks, thereby symbolizing the resurrection and coming of Christ in glory. So, according to this ancient ritual pattern, the new and decisive baptismal moment was when the newly baptized in Ravenna was faced by Christ and came to see his graced and gracing form. This was the moment, to return to our reflection on Michelangelo's painting in the Sistine Chapel, when the fingers meet, and regenerating grace was discharged.

How God's grace works on us in making us Christian is a crucial point, and in addressing this question we could draw an analogy with the work of a wood-polisher and say that baptismal grace works in the same way as the wood-polisher works with, and not against, the grain of the material he is polishing. By extension, then, we could say that God's grace works with the grain of our humanity, drawing out its particular features and making it shine, as Ambrose of Milan graphically put it, through the baptismal anointing. God's grace continues to work on us as we practice our Christian lives, but the sacramental action of baptism remains the definitive and unrepeatable influence in the formation of Christian character. For, following the model presented in the baptisteries at Ravenna, it is through baptism that a person is aligned to the figure of Christ who, as the New Testament testifies, is the pattern of our own formation as Christians. How we conceive this, as Hans Urs von Balthasar says in his colossal work of theological aesthetics *The Glory of the Lord* (1982), requires some theological imagination, and addressing the subject of the formative effect of baptism, von Balthasar uses the German word Einbildungskraft. This term is one of those complex German constructions combining a number of words, and literally means the "power to shape an image." In the context of the discussion the image referred to is Christ and the power is the Holy Spirit. So, in combining these two terms von Balthasar presents the meaning of baptism as the sacramental means whereby we are shaped by the Spirit according to the likeness of Christ.

The conceptualization of this idea in Balthasar's writing is abstruse and perhaps too abstract to comprehend, but what he is articulating can be pictured, and can be seen if we resume our virtual tour and return to the setting of baptism in Ravenna, imagining how it worked there; that is, how the rite might have been celebrated and the effect it had on its participants. Emerging from the water the candidate would thrust their head back, gasp for air, open their eyes and then see the epiphany of "the human form of God" in the figure of Christ. The combination of the enacted ritual and the visual artistic form conspire to create a truly performative art, for that moment (the baptism of Jesus) is happening now for the one who emerges from the baptismal pool. In a scholarly article on the mosaic of the Neonian Baptistery, A. J. Wharton (1987) argues that during the celebration of the rite of baptism, a truly "participative art" occurred in the sacred space beneath the baptistery dome. For what the candidate undergoes in the water-washing is both modeled upon and informed by the visual image of the baptism of Jesus by John in the River Jordan. (Incidentally, in the venerable Coptic tradition of Egypt, the font—the place of baptism—is called "the Jordan," an appellation that we might take as a cultural trace showing that the event of Jesus' baptism by John in the River Jordan is paradigmatic for our interpretation of what transpires through the liturgical celebration of baptism.) But, returning to the scene in Ravenna, we can say that in the moment of that live epiphany, the candidate would recognize that what they had undergone was what had happened to Jesus at the Jordan, that they were now identified with Jesus. With such a "recognition" would dawn the realization that they too were "beloved of God," the object of God's delight, and that they themselves were drawn to share in the filial experience which Jesus had with the Father. Furthermore, reading the artistic motif of the dove alongside the divine declaration "Thou art my beloved Son," one can see that through the bestowal of the spirit of adoption, the baptized were able to cry, as Jesus did: "Abba, Father," and articulate a longing for the coming of the fullness of the Kingdom of God. For in the celebration of the sacramental act faith is met by revelation, our seeking of God is answered by the disclosure of God in our human likeness, and in the performance of the rite, the participants find themselves enacting the reality they are participating in (the filial relationship of Jesus to the Father). And as we learn from the Greek theological tradition from Maximus the Confessor to Gregory Palamas, what we participate in becomes part of who we are, and literally informs our sense of identity. What we participate in is the life of Christ and we become Christ, are "rendered like him," as Gregory says, through the grace in the bath of regeneration; and having undergone a triple immersion in the water, which he takes as representing the three days in which Christ was in Hades, the newly baptized emerge as "the first fruits of resurrection" and as children of the light (cf. Ephesians 5:14).

Personal identity, the question of who and what we are, is inextricably bound up with the question of to whom we belong; when we unravel the meaning of baptism, we see that it is not only about our being identified with Christ, but also about our incorporation into a community, his Body, the Church. This vital aspect of the meaning of baptism as incorporation into the Body of Christ, of our being drawn into and given a place within the company of God's people, is also shown artistically in the dome mosaics of the baptisteries in Ravenna.

In the second register of artistic decoration, surrounding the roundel, the baptized are invited to step out and join the apostolic company of the Church as it is drawn into the eschatological age. What we see are two processions, figures of crown-bearing apostles moving in both directions, interspersed with date-palms laden with fruit. One procession is led by Peter (shown holding the keys) and the other by Paul (shown holding a manuscript of the Word). The image of the crown, often associated with the martyrs (those who have been victorious in the struggle), is also the symbol of the eschatological gift of life eternal—the "crown of life" or "crown of righteousness" (see Revelation 2:10; 2 Timothy 4:8)—making the procession a movement towards and into the fullness of life. This double dancing procession converges on the empty throne marked with the cross, the emblem of the crucified and risen Christ, identifying him as the one who at the end of time will judge the living and the dead. So, having been baptized, the neophytes (as they were called), probably now clothed in their white robes and bearing newly kindled lamps as newborn children of the resurrection, find themselves caught up quite literally in the apostolic dance into the presence and place of encounter with Christ, as they join a procession from the baptistery building into the main body of the church building, where the faithful are ready to greet them, and with whom they will celebrate the Eucharist together. In one sense this joining with others to celebrate the Eucharist represents the completion of their staged ritual of initiation into the Church; but then, as indeed now, it is important to see the wider perspective and recognize that each local worshipping community represents the wider and universal body of the Church. Again, as the mosaic figures of dancing apostles and the symbolic insignia of the saints of God indicate in the Ravenna baptistery decoration, the newly baptized are incorporated into the whole Church, visible and invisible, the living with the departed (who continue, as Paul, said "in the Lord"), and are enfolded into the one Body, the Church. In taking their place within the local worshipping community the baptized are enveloped into that single and therefore unifying Body of Christ, with the whole Communion of Saints, with whom we are caught up in that corporate eucharistic act of praise: "Therefore, with angels and archangels, and with all the company of heaven . . . ."

But to speak of the Eucharist is to anticipate the journey a bit, and we need to get back into line, to rejoin, as it were, the procession of the newly baptized as it enters the nave, in order to gather another point regarding their incorporation into the Body of Christ. Through the ritual path of this procession, the newly baptized join the body of worshippers gathered in the nave, and there are welcomed as children of God, a status that they themselves have received as a gift, freely donated and bestowed by God, in and through the Spirit. But what of those who are already gathered and waiting to welcome the newly baptized? How are they to receive them? Again, what it means to welcome the newly baptized is best spoken of in terms of "gift." As the newly baptized enter the nave, they are to be welcomed as gift, received by the body of worshippers as a bodily sign of that ultimate gift, the self-gift of Christ to the disciples at the Last Supper—"This, my body"—on which occasion the Eucharist, which together they are about to celebrate, was instituted. Moreover, through the celebration of the Eucharist, the place where they have gathered, the nave, will become the place where the Church, as the Body of Christ, will again come into being.

The Eucharist as celebrated in the fifth- and sixth-century churches of Ravenna would have been a highly stylized celebration incorporating elements of imperial court ceremonial. But those who gathered then, as those who gather at all times and places to make Eucharist, were called to be church. The Greek word in the New Testament for church is ekklesia, and it denotes not a gathering together as a group of like-minded people might gather, but those who are called together by God, and called to manifest the Church, that universal and disparate body of people, different in age, race, sexuality, experience, needs and background, who are drawn together by God to reveal the lineaments of a new humanity being made in Christ, in whom there is neither Jew nor Greek, slave nor free, male nor female (see Galatians 3:28; Romans 10:12). But how can these discrete and different bodies become this body? In other words, just how can an aggregate of diverse individuals become a single, unified body?

To begin to answer this question we need to move on in our virtual tour of Ravenna to the church of St. Apollinare Nuovo, built as the chapel for the Emperor Theodoric's palace, and consecrated in 504. It was originally dedicated to the honor of St. Martin of Tours, and apparently known as St. Martin in Heaven on account of its glittering mosaic decoration.

Again, we can begin to see an answer to these questions as we contemplate the mosaics that surround the space in which the people of God gathered together to celebrate the Eucharist. As we look at the nave, what we see are three decorated zones—on either side of the nave, moving towards the sanctuary—where the altar and bishop's throne are located. The first and lowest panel, directly above the arcade of pillars, shows a stately procession of saints; in the second band individual saints are depicted between the clerestory windows, and above this is the third zone of mosaic panels, thirteen on the north side showing gospel miracle scenes, and the same number on the south side showing scenes of Christ's passion. It should be noted, however, that this latter zone of mosaics does not actually depict the crucifixion. The motif of the "suffering Christ" did not become a central one of Christianity until after the first millennium of Christian history. This was not because previous generations wanted to deny Christ's physical suffering, or suppress the scandal of the cross, but living as they did in a more symbolic cultural world, the suffering and death of Christ were subsumed within a wider complex and interlocked pattern of symbolic representation.

Hence the mosaic of the Last Supper in this series (see p. 114), the first on the south wall, depicts Christ and the disciples lying, Roman style, around a table on which stands a plate containing two large fish. The earliest Christian graffiti, from the time of the persecutions in Rome, shows how the fish had become a sign of Christ, because the Greek word for fish (ichthys) is an acronym of "Jesus Christ, Son of God." So, the fish symbol of this mosaic panel of the Last Supper denoted Christ. But note that it was the whole mystery and fate of Christ's person that is symbolically depicted, that is, the very form of God in human form. But how is that essential "form of Christ" to be visually represented? The question, though a real one, is also rhetorical as it contains in itself the hint of the answer, namely in that whatever we might know about God, we know that God seeks to communicate himself, to bring himself to self-expression through the Word. We can only begin to speak of God because he reveals himself; but as with all revelations, this self-revelation of God in Christ is at one and the same time both a disclosure and a concealment, and so cannot be visually displayed in any straightforward or transparent way. Hence the symbolic depiction. The fish denotes Christ, but in this panel it triggers a whole range of connotations. The figure of Jesus is shown with his right hand in blessing over the table of bread and fish, and is the closest of the passion series to the altar, at which the bishop, or presiding priest at a celebration of the Eucharist, would make the sign of the cross over the bread and wine, offered to commemorate Christ's death and passion. The siting of these images is significant, and the proximity of this mosaic panel to the altar signals the close link between the Last Supper and the celebration of the Eucharist. Directly opposite, on the north wall of the nave, the mosaic depicts Christ changing the water into wine at the marriage feast in Cana of Galilee. So, these two panels, the Last Supper and the Cana mosaic, sited at the east end of the nave, form a kind of iconic frame inviting us to see the Lord's Supper as a transformative event effected by Christ's very giving of himself. In receiving that gift sacramentally in the Eucharist, we become again what we have been made at baptism, and it is that ritual transaction of the glorious exchange between God and humanity that we must consider in the following chapter.

6
Becoming What You Receive

At the outset of the previous chapter I suggested that the economy of salvation, that is, God's offer of salvation and how we might receive and appropriate that gift, was transacted bodily in a ritual pattern of mutual giving and receiving. These bodily transactions occur in the context of liturgical celebrations, and again, we can see part of what this means when we contemplate the mosaic schemes in the sacred places in Ravenna. In particular, when we look again at the mosaic panel of the Last Supper sited closest to the altar on the south wall of the nave of St. Apollinare Nuovo, we see that although what is offered and received at the Eucharist is freely set before us, it is of an incalculable cost to God. As the prophet's announcement of God's offer of salvation makes clear, God's generosity is incomparable: "Come, buy and eat! . . . Buy without money and without price!" (Isaiah 55:1; compare Proverbs 9:8, telling how Wisdom sets her table and offers the promise of life). What God offers is pure gift and can never be earned or bought by us. But the cost to God is none other than the life of his Son: "Sparing not his own Son, God gave him up for us all" (Romans 8:32).

When we look at the mosaic of the Last Supper we see the figure of Christ with the disciples gathered around a table bearing a plate on which are placed two fish; the Passover meal is transposed, for the traditional Jewish Passover lamb becomes two fish. The emblem of the fish is a condensed symbol, layering and compressing together a number of gospel images and meanings. It evokes the miracle of the feeding of the multitude with the five loaves and the two fish, an episode exhibiting the advent of God with humankind, and also recalls the story of the appearance by the lake of the risen Christ who summoned the disciples to a breakfast of fish. But preeminently the fish, as we have seen, represents Christ himself, and so what this particular Last Supper mosaic shows is that what Christ offers to his disciples is his own self, and what the disciples receive is none other than Christ's gift of himself and a share in his own being and life. In this way the mosaic shows us the

The Last Supper Mosaic, St. Apollinaire Nuovo, Ravenna

eucharistic grammar of giving and receiving, and in using the symbol of the fish—condensing as it does the appearing of God's presence with humankind (as in the feeding miracle), the passion and death of Christ, and our eating and drinking with the risen Christ—reveals that the eucharistic gifts are multivalent and charged with significance. No wonder, then, that the Eucharist came to be considered to be *the* icon of Christ, revealing as it does, the very "form of Christ."

John's account of the Last Supper opens with a summary comment of the drama that is to unfold, saying that Christ "loved his own . . . to the end."

The end was the free giving of himself, and it was this sacrificial act of self-giving that was prefigured in the giving of the bread and cup at the Last Supper. With the words "Take, eat" Christ hands himself over to the disciples before he is "handed over" to be crucified. The final handing over, of course, is the total giving of himself to the Father on the cross of Calvary, thus making the giving and receiving of the eucharistic bread the sacramental means whereby the disciples themselves are drawn into Christ's ultimate self-giving to the Father on the cross of Calvary. Thus we see just how costly Communion is, for what we receive is the cost of sacrifice, calling from those who receive the gifts an answering sacrifice in the giving of "ourselves, our souls and bodies." The sacrifice of Christ has its counterpoint in the thankful offering of ourselves. Indeed, as we reflect further on the liturgical theology of the Ravenna mosaics, we increasingly see how the drama of salvation, ritually enacted in sacramental celebrations, is neither divorced from the historical reality of Christ Jesus, nor from the temporal contingencies of our corporeal existence.

The mosaic panels in the upper register above the clerestory windows in St. Apollinare Nuovo, are sometimes read as a precursor of the stained-glass *sacrae historiae* of the later Middle Ages. There might well be a line of development to be traced here, but the mosaic ensemble is not simply, in Gregory the Great's often quoted words, intended as "books for the illiterate," or simply a visual illustration of the oral proclamation of the gospel. Aidan Kavanagh's account that "what the viewers saw is what they heard" (1990, p. 268), as if they were intended as gospel illustrations, is a rather 115 limited explanation, and quite frankly unlikely. For the details of these gospel mosaic scenes (as is also true of the gospel scene mosaics in the prestigious late fourth- and fifth-century Roman churches of St. Paul Outside the Walls and St. Maria Maggiore) are illegible to the unassisted eye. In comparison with the scale of the building, the panels are small, and their positioning above the level of the clerestory windows means that they are not conveniently placed for immediate visibility. So what was the intention of placing these small panels here? How else might we account for their place and function? I would argue that what we see here is an instance of iconic, or sacramental, art.

What I mean by this is that they "make present" the form of Christ in figurative form, in the very space in which the worshippers have gathered to be reconfigured to the form of Christ through the ritual enactment of the Eucharist. This iconic art seen in Rome and Ravenna, came to be reproduced north of the Alps, and one stunning example can still be seen in the ninth-century monastic church of St. George at Oberzell, on Reichenau, a small island on Lake Constance, which forms part of the border between Germany and Switzerland. Although the church is heavily restored, a series of painted frescoes depicting the works of Christ, with captions beneath each scene, survives on the walls of the nave, representing an artistic arrangement that one can reasonably suppose was fairly widespread throughout the Romanesque period of church building and decoration.

This artistic genre is highly significant, both theologically and liturgically. First, theologically, the showing of the figure of Christ is a testimony to the fact that the Christ is not an abstract idea, or a kind of heavenly projection of the "perfect man," but is inseparable from the historical figure of Jesus of Nazareth: a figure, as shown by the Gospel writers, who was circumscribed by particular encounters and defined by the contents of his proclamation, his particular words and actions, which brought to expression and embodied the coming Kingdom of God. In terms of the liturgy, the artistic figuring of Christ on the walls of the nave signals the fact that the Christ who calls people to his table, and in whom Christians are incorporated (literally, made part of his Body), is the figure of Jesus Christ.

The linkage between the theological and liturgical points I have drawn out here was famously spelled out in a sermon of the fifth-century by Pope Leo the Great. The sermon in question was preached on the Feast of the Ascension, and as with all attempts at expounding the Easter mystery, Leo finds himself up against the inescapable notion of the divine *absence.* The angelic announcement on Easter morning signals this divine absence: "He is not here; he is risen!" an absence which attracts a certain finality in Luke's narrative of the ascension in the first chapter of the Acts of the Apostles, and is poignantly preserved in the ancient Coptic tradition in which the Feast of the Ascension is called the "leave taking." In his sermon, Pope Leo acknowledged the fact of the physical absence of Jesus, but went on to assert that what had been visible in the redeemer has passed over into the mysteries, that is, into the sacramental celebrations of the Church. This saying came to be a basic maxim in the liturgical theology of the Early Church Fathers, and later was taken up by Thomas Aquinas (1225–1274) and written into his compendious systematic theology. The same conviction has been restated more recently by Edward Kilmartin (1998, p. 317). He argued that what was mediated in the liturgy was none other than the work and fate of Christ Jesus, and insisted that there was no power in the liturgy that was not identifiable with the concrete historic actions and passions of Jesus Christ.

What this underscores is that the One who calls us together, and who meets us in the unfolding drama of the celebration of the Eucharist, is the very One of whom the Gospels bear witness: Jesus of Nazareth. It is, in other words, the historic Christ Jesus, whose individual encounters with people in Galilee and Jerusalem 2,000 years ago, is the same Christ who encounters worshippers in the contemporary "holy theatre" of our sacramental celebrations. For in the context of an actual liturgical celebration, space and location elide, and what transpired there, occurs here. It is as though the coordinates of time—present, past and future—coincide in a distended liturgical time, making that which is artistically shown as occurring in time past, happen now. Quite simply, this liturgical art conspires to show that the place we gather for worship is the place and the occasion of our encounter with Christ. Each of the scenes depicted in the gospel mosaics, then, does not show an isolated wonder of the gospel, locked in an irretrievable past, but is iconic and makes visible a presence. Moreover, they not only mediate a presence, but identify the One who is making himself present in and through those gathered in the defined space as Jesus Christ. The sacramental "coming to presence" of Christ in the enacted celebration is a presence played out in different modes, as he comes to be present in his Word, in the breaking of bread, and in the persons of the baptized who gather in the place of encounter in order to be made again one body in Christ.

The gospel mosaic panels in the upper register of decorations in the nave of St. Apollinare Nuovo, present us with a number of gospel truths. One can only guess at what determined the choice of these particular scenes from the four Gospels of the New Testament. But it is intriguing to see that what was chosen and shown in this liturgical art effectively brings the *practice* of Christian life to light. So let us briefly look at some specific examples and see something of the content of what is brought to light. One of the panels shows Jesus meeting the Samaritan woman at the well. The narrative account of this encounter recorded in John's Gospel is very telling. It is Jesus who initiates the conversation, disregarding the conventional social barriers that separated people on grounds of race, religion and gender. As the exchange between Jesus and the Samaritan woman unfolds, so the truth becomes transparent; the basis of this woman's relationships is laid bare as she is confronted by the Christ and she finally learns that the true God is worshipped in and through the Spirit. Here, then, is the fact that when we encounter Christ he confronts us with the truth about ourselves and exposes where and how we face and meet others. The face of Christ in these gospel mosaics is both compassionate and searching and, like the Samaritan woman, as we come to the place of prayer we too are faced by Christ: his challenging gaze scrutinizes where and how we stand in our relationships. Some of the gospel mosaics present the Christ who addresses issues of wealth and status, and we see how a searching light is cast on the invidious ways we set ourselves apart from others and gain an advantage over them. Others, such as the scene of the poor woman whom Jesus observed placing her small coin in offering, make visible those who in our own eyes go unnoticed and unrecognized. So, the question of how we face and meet others is paramount and one that seems bound up with how we think we stand in relation to God. Unsurprisingly, we see included in this artistic scheme a mosaic of the parable of the pharisee and the publican. The gospel truth that shines out here is the challenge not to define ourselves by drawing comparisons between ourselves and others, but honestly to face ourselves and acknowledge our own need for the healing mercy of God. Ultimately, of course, as the mosaic of the separation of the sheep and the goats reminds us, we are judged on the scale of gospel values, and what counts is a life that generously gives itself to others, a life that seeks justice and exhibits acts of practical kindness and care.

Reviewing the whole scheme of gospel mosaics, significantly situated in the very place where Christians gather for the celebration of the Eucharist, we could say that the Christ who calls the worshipper, and who makes himself present for them, calls them also to a particular way of life, a living out of that gospel which comes to expression in the celebration of the liturgy. Our Christian life is formed in and through the liturgy, but liturgy and life are indivisible—each must weave in and out of the other if we are to come truly to live out of our worship.

Returning to the particularly liturgical focus of our exploration, we can see that three vitally related elements are emerging from our virtual view of the sacred space of St. Apollinare Nuovo. The first is the liturgical artwork; the second, the worshippers gathered in the architectural space of the nave; and third, the actual ritual enactment that takes place there. These three elements interact with each other to such an extent that they form a single ensemble, in which each element relates to, and informs, the other two. So, for instance, our reflections above regarding the gospel mosaics panels show a correspondence between that element of the liturgical art and the body of worshippers. But the aspect we must now consider is the relation between this element of the liturgical art and the ritual celebration of the Eucharist. It is my contention that as the liturgical art works in the baptisteries of Ravenna by showing the meaning of baptism as it is ritually enacted, so the nave mosaics of St. Apollinare come alive, as we might say, during the celebration of the Eucharist. As we have seen, what is depicted in gospel scene mosaics is the entire Christ, and in this we can see a correspondence between the mosaic artwork and the great Prayer of Thanksgiving (now generally called the Eucharistic Prayer). For as the artwork makes visible the whole Christ—i.e., the teaching and healing Christ, the suffering Christ and the risen and glorified Christ—so it is the whole Christ who is commemorated in the Eucharistic Prayer. In this respect, the gospel mosaics constitute a visual parallel to that particular section of the Eucharistic Prayer known as the *anamnesis,* the verbal memorial of Christ, following immediately after the words of institution in which the celebrant rehearses the words spoken by Jesus over the bread and cup at the Last Supper. The overall effect of the celebration in this setting, then, is for the various elements, the solemnly recited words of the Eucharistic Prayer, the worshippers gathered in the architectural space, the bread and the cup on the altar, and the surrounding visual images, to correspond with each other and interlock in an intricate network of sacred signs which together designate "the Body of Christ," the new temple, the intersection of time and eternity, and the place where the divine and human coincide.

This view of liturgical celebration is inspired by the liturgical artwork of the sacred sites of the ancient Christian center, Ravenna, a city which in terms of ecclesiastical prestige vied with Ambrose's city of Milan and ranked second below Rome and Constantinople, the respective centers of the Western and Eastern Christian worlds. It reflects the dynamic liturgical theology that characterized the Patristic era, and that was partly recovered by the movement of liturgical renewal during the past century across the ecumenical spectrum of Churches. But this is at risk of being obscured again as we give priority to the shape and structure of the liturgy over the form and content of liturgical celebration (of what we do, and what might transpire if we open ourselves to what is promised in the liturgy). Admittedly, the fifth- and sixth-century churches and baptisteries of Ravenna belong to a very different world from our own; we cannot culturally relocate ourselves and I am not suggesting that we reconstruct our places of worship according to those ancient models and decorative schemes. The past is more than a foreign country—it is largely a lost country. But the vestiges of Christian culture we have seen in Ravenna are traces of an understanding of what the liturgy means that can indeed challenge our own liturgical attitudes and open up new or forgotten perspectives. In our own times, for instance, when we tend to tend to think of liturgy as texts for worship, it is important to recognize the wider context, including the physical setting in which it takes place and, equally significant, the actual worshipping community that celebrates it. Again, in our own context where we tend to view worship in terms of our own work—whether it is constructing a so-called "creative liturgy" or of being a skilled "worship leader"—and to evaluate our experience of worship in terms of its subjective effect upon us, it might be salutary to recall a more objective view of liturgy in order to shift our perspective away from what we do in worship to seeing in it the action of that Other whom we call God, who wills to work on and through us. It is precisely in this way that the liturgical art of Ravenna can inform our appreciation of what might occur in the event of a liturgical celebration.

Further, our virtual tour of the liturgical art in Ravenna locates the meaning of the sacraments in the context of celebrated liturgical rites, which not only precludes an instrumental view regarding them as "things" to be dispensed as if God could be at our disposal, but invites us to see God in these celebrations as the hidden actor, drawing and reconfiguring us to be Christ's Body. This is not to cast the worshipper into the passive role of spectator however; far from it. Something vital is required of the worshipper, which we might cautiously call our "cooperation." What I mean by cooperation is more than consent, our "Amen" if you like. It is an active working together with Christ, but a working that must spring from that contemplative attitude that I have described as a receptive attentiveness to what is said and done in the performance of the liturgy. It is such an attitude alone that can make us truly present to the Christ who encounters us in the Word and the sacramental signs of his very being and life.

What the liturgical theology of Ravenna shows is that what worshippers become is none other than Christ himself. Baptism incorporates us into Christ, making us members of his Body the Church, which is realized anew at each celebration of the Eucharist. The Eucharist makes the Church, and through the body of worshippers, Christ is located in and for the world. For the One who is iconographically present in the gospel scene mosaics, is the One with whom they are increasingly identified through the unfolding celebration of the sacred mysteries. And what unfolds in those liturgical acts is the unfolding of the "mystery of God's purpose" (Ephesians 1:9–10), that remaking of humanity in making us one body, to be the leavening presence of Christ in human society. The meaning is deeply layered, and as each layer of meaning refers back to the celebration of the Eucharist, we might say that the Eucharist not only makes the Church, but also remakes humanity. How this might actually work requires us to think particularly about how a specific group of people celebrating the Eucharist in a particular time and place are drawn into its meaning. As we have seen, the Eucharist is essentially the *anamnesis* of Christ, the remembering or commemoration, of the whole Christ, incarnate, crucified and glorified. Those who faithfully participate in this solemn act might undergo a corresponding kind of *anamnesis*, a remembering of themselves as the Body of Christ. Indeed, each and every celebration of the Eucharist can be for those who celebrate it the occasion for "remembering" which, being the opposite of what is denoted by that vicious term "dismember," entails a putting "back together again." In other words, the celebration of the Eucharist can be the occasion when we remember who we really are and are put together. In the liturgical context this remembering of who we are occurs in the corporate setting of the Eucharist, thereby grounding our identity in relation to others in the one Body of the Church: "we being many, are one bread, one body, because we all partake of the one bread" (1 Corinthians 10:16). Through the sacramental body, we might say, we discover that we belong to one another; we come to find and define ourselves in relationship with others within the Body of Christ.

The way the New Testament metaphor of the "body" continuously seems to slip and slide across the three referents of the eucharistic elements of bread and wine, the social body of the Church and the figure of Jesus Christ produces a puzzling conundrum. We have already looked at the question of how "this body" (the baptized) becomes part of "that body" (Jesus Christ) through the ritual enactment of baptism. But how might "that body" (the body of Jesus) be "those bodies" (the body of Christians)? The puzzle, of course, is as old as Christianity itself. Indeed, we might recall the story of the dazzling appearance of Christ to Paul as he traveled along the road to Damascus to persecute the members of the Way (as Christians were first called). On that occasion Christ faced him with the question: "Saul, why are you persecuting me?" (Acts 9:1–6). The question is not "Why are you persecuting them?" but "Why are you persecuting me?" Christ so identifies himself with the Church that it becomes his Body, and so Paul the persecutor, in harassing the social body of Christians, is violating the very body of Jesus.

This linguistic play between referents, the body of Jesus and the social body of Christians, is especially evident in discussions about the Eucharist, and from earliest times received the attention of prominent Christian thinkers and teachers. In his preaching, Augustine of Hippo, for instance, urged the faithful to "Be what you *see; receive* what you are" (Sermon 227), and in even more startling language spoke of how the recipient is identified with the very gift: "what you receive is the mystery that means you. It is to what you are that you reply *Amen*" (Sermon 272). In explicating this exhortation, commentators have rightly underlined the emphasis on the sheer gratuitousness of God's repeated self-gift in the Eucharist, and have seen our participation in the Eucharist as the means whereby we assimilate and become what we are enabled to be through baptism, namely, the Body of Christ. In one passage in his *Confessions,* Augustine comes remarkably close to the Eastern understanding of *theosis,* or divinization, where, in speaking of the transformation effected by the Eucharist, he places these words into the mouth of Christ: "you shall not change Me into yourself as bodily food, but into Me you shall be changed" (Book VII.X.16). In the case of our sacramental eating and drinking, we become what we eat.

What intrigues me about the language in Augustine's Sermon 227 is the visual reference and the implied correlation between *seeing* and our *becoming* what God wants us to be: "be what you *see.*" This expression neatly gathers up the points we have previously made about how the form of Christ was revealed to those being baptized, and of how the small mosaic panels along the north and south walls of the nave of St. Apollinare Nuovo, are a visual *anamnesis,* an iconic "making-present" of Christ for those who celebrate the liturgy as the people of God. The meaning of what happens in the celebration of baptism and Eucharist is shown in the mosaic artwork and assimilated by the worshippers as they participate in the rites enacted in the ambiance of the sacred space. The artwork of both baptistery and nave becomes a visual montage, revealing what it is to be baptized and to be incorporated into Christ. The baptized themselves are informed by the "human form divine" and as they come to the Eucharist they are identified, and identified with increasing intensity as the ritual action unfolds, with "this body," the Body of Christ. That body, first revealed to them as the human form of God in the dome of the baptistery, then identified as the Jesus whose words and actions are iconically presented in the mosaic gospel panels, is the One who constitutes them as his body as they join and interact with other worshippers in the nave of the basilica.

What our reflections on the rite as celebrated in the sacred spaces of Ravenna have shown (one might even say revealed) is that the sacred space of worship is the place where, with others, the people of God can orientate themselves towards God, and receive that which gives their lives both direction and depth, as they come to embody Christ, and then body him forth in the embodied exchanges of their ordinary lives. Such an identification might well strike us as being a rather audacious claim, but consider the bold language used by Cyril of Jerusalem, who when addressing the newly baptized, told them that through their anointing with the oil of chrism "you were made Christs" and "icons of Christ" (*Mystagogical Catecheses* III.1). Furthermore, through the sacramental eating and drinking of the Eucharist gifts of Christ's very being and life, the Christian can again be "Christed," renewed in his image, and more closely shaped after his likeness. Quite simply, through our sharing in the Eucharist we can become again what we were made at baptism.

Another more recent historical trace of the conviction that the physical bodies of Christians are to be identified with the Body of Christ is found in Cranmer's service for the solemnization of marriage. This is a rather unexpected source, but the significance of the context should not have surprised us, as one cannot imagine a more literal bodily exchange and identification than the physical intimacy of two bodies becoming one flesh. The final rubric in Cranmer's rite in the 1549 and 1552 Prayer Books emphatically directs that: "The newe married persons (the same day of their marriage) must receive the holy communion." (The direction is softened somewhat in the corresponding rubric in the rite of the 1662 Prayer Book which speaks of it being convenient for the newly married persons to receive Communion at the time of their marriage, or at the first opportunity!) Although Cranmer would not cast the matter in terms of our argument about bodily identification, what we have in this historical example is a vestigial insight, that if a loving relationship between two people is to be an icon of the mystery of the union of Christ with his Church (the sacramental reality of Christian marriage), then their bodies need to embody Christ. Again, it is a question of this, of these bodies becoming part of that Body, the single Body of Christ.

How might this happen? The question of how the disparate social Body of worshippers might be transformed into the single and unified Body of Christ can be illustrated by uncovering the underlying structure and narrative flow of the Eucharistic Prayer. Looking behind the words and tracing the direction of what is being said in that prayer, we can see that what the prayer intends is that those who are joined to Christ through baptism might themselves become the very bearers of Christ. So let us look at the Eucharistic Prayer itself and its intention of making the eucharistic Body.

The Eucharist Prayer begins with the opening dialogue, "The Lord be with you. *And also with you,*" a mutual recognition that the Lord is present with those who have gathered to celebrate, both president and people, and reaches its climax with a doxology, an ascription of praise by those who are "in Christ": "Through him, and with him, and in him," So from the beginning of that prayer to its climax of praise, sealed by the common *Amen,* there is an explicit recognition that Christians are incorporated into Christ. While the structure of that prayer unfolds, the worshippers are progressively reconfigured to the figure of Christ, as that figure is drawn in the prayer's recital of God's saving deeds and given a voice in the words of the institution narrative: "this, my body," "this, my blood." Looking at the Eucharistic Prayer in this way, we can see that the plot of the story of salvation recited in the prayer transports those who say and pray the prayer from being "in Christ" to the end point, indicated by the words "Take, and eat it. . . . drink this all of you," which is "Christ being in us." The worshippers are implicated, involved and carried along, through the repeated "we" in the prayer voiced by the president as the narrative of the prayer unfolds and are propelled by its flow towards the point of Christ becoming present in the communicants through the act of Communion. The prayer, once taken as a hallmark of Anglican liturgy, "We do not presume to come to this your table," is placed immediately before the distribution of Communion in *Common Worship,* and enunciates the hope of fruitful communion, that the communicants may "dwell in him and he in us." This is the point to which the narrative flow of the Eucharistic Prayer carries us, its destination. So it is, quite simply, through Christ's indwelling us that we, though many, can be made *one* Body and find ourselves bonded together in a reconfiguration of relationships which is the new Covenant.

The view of the act of receiving Communion as the occasion when Christ comes to dwell within his people has a number of antecedents in the Western liturgical tradition. The Advent Collect in the seventh-century *Gelasian Sacramentary* (a collection of seasonal prayer texts for the Mass in Rome) asks that our consciences may be so cleansed that Christ, at his coming, may find in us a dwelling place. This theme of Christ's indwelling is now found in a number of official *Common Worship* texts, such as the collect for Christmas Day, the post-communion prayer for the second Sunday after Christmas, and the propers provided for a Dedication Festival. The linkage between Christ indwelling his people and the Eucharist is grounded in the "Bread of Life" discourse in chapter 6 of John's Gospel, and was taken up to became a major theme in the eucharistic theology of the English Reformer, Thomas Cranmer. In the consecration prayer of his first English Prayer Book of 1549, we find the line asking that those who are to receive Communion may be "made one bodye with thy sonne Jesu Christ, that he may dwell in them, and they in him." Similarly, in a prayer beautifully crafted by Bishop Lancelot

Andrewes to be said privately after the Prayer of Consecration, the intending communicant asks "that we may have Christ dwelling in our hearts." This theme of Christ's indwelling through the act of Communion could well be regarded as a particular Anglican emphasis, so it is gratifying to see it emerge as a theme in the *Common Worship* collects for the commemoration of the sixteenth- and seventeenth-century Anglican Divines, Richard Hooker and Jeremy Taylor.

Liturgical revision brings its gains and its losses, but even the latter can be instructive. As Bridget Nichols (1996) has shown in her incisive analysis of liturgical language and interpretation, the sense of Christ's "indwelling through Communion" was lost in the English translation of the people's response to the invitation to Communion in the Roman Missal of 1973. A slightly adapted form of this was adopted as an alternative invitation to Communion in the Church of England's *Alternative Service Book 1980,* and its fairly widespread use secured its inclusion in *Common Worship* (1998): "Jesus is the Lamb of God. . . . Happy are those who are called to his supper." This declaration associates the eucharistic gifts with the heavenly banquet, declaring it to be a foretaste, an antipasto, we might say, of the eschatological marriage feast of the Lamb (see Revelation 19:9–10). In the Latin text of the modern Roman rite, the congregation's response to the invitation to Communion faithfully echoes the protestation of the Roman centurion to Jesus, as he made his way to the official's house to attend to the sick servant (see Luke 7:01–10; Matthew 8:5–13): "Domine, non sum dignus ut intres sub tectum meum" ("Lord, I am not worthy for you to come under my roof"). The modern English rendering of this response slants and narrows its meaning by focusing on the actual reception of the consecrated elements: "Lord, I am not worthy to *receive* you." The omission of the words "under my roof " removes at one stroke the connotation of dwelling, of Christ coming to "abide" in us, and places the emphasis on our act of receiving. Perhaps the linguistic adjustments reflect wider cultural influences, with a hint of contemporary consumerism (with its preoccupation with what we "get") and our culture of suspicion; specifically, the suspicion pervading our individualistic society of another intruding into the guarded domain of the private and autonomous "self." I happen to be writing this during a stay in the Benedictine Abbey at Trier, and was pleased to see that the German translation retains this reference, which is not only a faithful echo of a gospel story, but enunciates that sense, characteristically expanded in the Byzantine version of this same prayer attributed to John Chrysostom, that Christ "wills to dwell in us."

But, as Louis-Marie Chauvet memorably puts it in his book *The Sacraments: The Word of God at the Mercy of the Body* (2001), "something else" is needed if Christ is to indwell his people, and if they are truly to reveal him and manifest his love and life to others through their own words, attitudes and actions. This "something else" is the operation of the Holy Spirit. Again, to pick up the terms of our earlier discussion of the interpretation of liturgical texts at the end of Chapter 4, we could say that the promise of what is proposed in liturgical texts (our transformation in Christ) can only be activated by the Spirit. The written letter proposes, but it is the Spirit that gives life. Before we look specifically at the place and role of the Spirit in the context of the celebration of the Eucharist, however, we need to make some remarks about how we might understand the working of the Spirit in relation to the self-body of our human nature.

The Holy Spirit, like the working of sacramental grace generally, never compels us nor overrides our wills but works, as we have suggested, with the very grain of our lives. For the Spirit, we are told, is Love (see John 4:24 and 1 John 4:8b) and as true love respects the difference of the other, and allows the other to be and to flourish, so the Spirit never manipulates nor flattens our unique individuality. As classical theology expounds, nature and grace are intrinsically related. What this means is that the gracious working of God needs to be met by a certain disposition and response on our part. The Spirit calls out: "will you, won't you, will you, won't you, join in the dance?" Our stepping out and moving to the rhythm of love is "faith," a faith that is characterized as a responsive openness and receptivity to God's gift and gracious working through the Spirit. Augustine insisted that the fruitful reception of Christ in Communion was correlated with (not dependent upon) the communicant's faith: "If you receive them well, you are yourselves what you receive" (Sermon 227). In his English Prayer Book, the Reformer Thomas Cranmer instructed those who intended to receive Communion to "Draw near with *faith*." But note that in the first instance our faith is awakened by God's grace, and the faith presupposed by Augustine is characterized as a receptive openness to God's gift, to his self-communication, which is none other than Christ himself, the divine Word.

In one of his splendid Eucharistic hymns Charles Wesley echoes a phrase from John's Gospel in speaking of the Holy Spirit as the "remembrancer of Christ," the One who draws out the significance of Christ's words, and realizes in our hearts and lives the effects of his saving work (see John 14:26). Earlier seventeenth-century Anglican Divines had also accorded a central place to the Spirit in the act of Communion. John Cosin (1594–1672), who played a key role in the restoration of the Church of England as the major draughtsman in the Prayer Book revision which led to the 1662 version of the Book of Common Prayer, argued in his polemical work against the Roman doctrine of eucharistic transubstantiation, that in Communion we truly participate in the body and blood of Christ, and that this effected the promised mutual indwelling of Christ (John 6:56). But such fruitful Communion, he stressed categorically, "is the operation of the Holy Spirit." The key role played by the Holy Spirit in the Eucharist had also been highlighted by Jeremy Taylor (1613–67). In his Holy Living (1650), he boldly informs the communicant that through the sacramental eating and drinking: "You have taken Christ into you." What he meant by this was explained in further detail in his *Worthy Communicant* (1660), where he argued that this sacramental conveyance of Christ to the communicant was the effect of Christ's Word *and* the work of the Holy Spirit. Indeed, there are repeated references to the Spirit throughout this work. Here, Taylor speaks specifically of the Holy Spirit in connection with the consecration of bread and wine and calls the Spirit "the consecrator of the mysteries" and "the glory of the change." But he is not wanting his reader to limit the Spirit to a particular moment in the celebration, or a particular formula in the Eucharistic Prayer, for the Spirit pervades the whole celebration, and in his view even the act of receiving Communion is to "partake of the Spirit." Indeed, the impression Taylor gives his reader is that the Spirit is the climate in which the Eucharist is celebrated, and the means through which the fruits of the Spirit—love, joy and peace (Galatians 5:22)—can come to maturity in our lives and relationships. This consideration of the Holy Spirit brings us to consider specifically that dimension or aspect of the Eucharistic Prayer that is technically known as the epiclesis, a Greek word meaning an invocation, asking that

God may be present and active in the liturgical rite. Today, the term is generally used to refer to a particular section of the Eucharistic Prayer asking God the Father to send the Holy Spirit. However, it seems that this element of invocation was so germane to the tradition of Thanksgiving Prayers (over bread and wine for the Eucharist, or water and oil for baptism) that some early Christian writers, such as Irenaeus, called the whole *anaphora* (Eucharistic Prayer), and not just a particular section of it, the *epiclesis* or invocation (see *Against the Heresies* 4.18.6; compare Basil of Caesarea, *The Holy Spirit* 27).

It is thought that the epicletal aspect of Thanksgiving Prayers has its distant origins in the religious practice of calling upon God's name to effect or release a blessing on a person, or specified object. In Hebrew thought, of course, the divine name was inseparably bound up with presence, and the royal psalms of Israel are full of invocations to YHWH to come into his holy temple. So, from forms of temple worship to the Christian thanksgiving, the *epiclesis* invokes the divine presence to make the offering holy and salvific for those who have a share and participate in it. But *who* exactly was invoked? Earliest references do not seem to differentiate between the Logos (the Word) and the Spirit, and the Greek-speaking Egyptian theological tradition often speaks of both being in tandem! Thus a liturgical fragment of a Eucharistic Prayer associated with the fourth-century bishop, Serapion of Egypt, invokes the Logos over the gifts of bread and wine: "O God of truth, let your holy Word come on this bread that the bread may become the bread of the Word. . . ."

The cautious historian would wisely say that the development of the *epiclesis* in fixed liturgical texts took a number of different tracks, reflecting a geographical variety of expression and understanding in the diverse centers of the Early Church. In the earliest extant fixed Eucharistic Prayer, known as the *Apostolic Tradition* and associated with Hippolytus of Rome, the *epiclesis* is addressed to the Father and asks God to *send* the Holy Spirit upon the offering, that is, on the whole act of giving thanks over the bread and the cup, in order that those who participate in it may be united in the one Body of Christ and confirmed in the truth of faith. Although scholars warn us that this is an uncertain and difficult text, we can reasonably adduce that the focus of the petition is on the worshippers, rather than on the bread and cup. The East

Syrian *Addai and Mari* Eucharistic Prayer, which in tone and vocabulary exhibits a distinctly Semitic influence and possibly reflects forms of prayer dating back to the first half of the second century, includes an *epiclesis* addressed to "the Lord" (Christ, the Son) and asks: "And let your Holy Spirit, O Lord, *come* and *rest* upon this offering of your servants." In this case, although the *epiclesis* is directly associated with the eucharistic gifts, the purpose of the invocation is not primarily the consecration of the elements of bread and wine, but that the communicants themselves might receive the fruits of Communion, in this instance, forgiveness, resurrection, and the new life of the Kingdom.

Early Syrian sources retain a strong eschatological sense, echoing the prayer of the earliest Christian assembly: *Marana' tha,* "Our Lord, Come!" (1 Corinthians 16:22; Revelation 22:20). Their acute sense of expectation of the coming of the Christ in glory and the fulfilling of God's purpose came to expression in their invocative prayers, the tone and orientation of which had already been set by the pattern and model of all Christian prayer, the Lord's Prayer: "Your kingdom *come;* your will be done on earth as it is in heaven." The imperative "come" has long been recognized as the most primitive term in the vocabulary of the liturgical *epiclesis* in the Syrian liturgical tradition and in Christian apocryphal literature, such as *The Acts of Thomas,* where we find a prayer simply calling on Christ to "come!" These prayer texts suggest an analogy between the epicletal character of the Eucharist and the Gospel accounts of Jesus' baptism by John in the River Jordan, which cast the Spirit in the role of the one who discloses or shows the reality of Christ's divine presence. The Spirit declares by showing, or manifesting, the appearing and parousia of the Christ. As a striking line in a West Syrian liturgical poem for the Feast of Pentecost, commemorating the sending of the Spirit upon the Church, says: "The Spirit declares, but cannot be expressed in language."

In later Eastern liturgical traditions, as witnessed to in the teaching of Cyril of Jerusalem to the newly baptized, and the *anaphoras* of the Byzantine rite, the *epiclesis* focuses explicitly upon the consecration, or the transformation of the bread and wine into the body and blood of Christ. Hence the technical term of "consecratory epiclesis" which Cyril explains in these terms:

> we call upon the merciful God to send forth his Holy Spirit upon the gifts lying before him; that he may make the bread the body of Christ, and the wine the blood of Christ; for whatever the Holy Spirit has touched, is sanctified and changed (*Mystagogical Catechesis* V.7).

This explanation, however, is partial and incomplete, because the evidence of the actual liturgical texts tends to the conclusion that even in the case of a fully blown consecratory *epiclesis,* the participants are implicated, for the very reason the eucharistic gifts are sanctified is that they might affect those who receive them, that the communicants themselves might be changed! This is the desired and prayed for outcome. Ultimately, then, the trajectory leads to a change or transformation being effected in those who participate in the sacramental celebration, and the metaphor of the sacramental body elides again with the metaphor of the worshippers as the Body of Christ.

In many of the contemporary Eucharistic Prayers, modeled as they are on the shape of the ancient Eucharistic Prayers of Antioch, the *epiclesis* is a *"double epiclesis,"* that is, an invocation of the Spirit on both the eucharistic gifts of bread and wine and upon the people. Structurally, this section of the prayer follows directly from the so-called *anamnesis,* that section of the prayer which, as we have seen in our discussion above, identifies the One who is commemorated in the Eucharist as the crucified, risen and glorified Jesus Christ. For how the past events of Christ's passion and his saving death and resurrection might bear on the present moment of eucharistic celebration depends upon the active presence of the Holy Spirit. As a fourteenth-century commentator on the divine liturgy, Nicholas Cabasilas, expressed it, the power to fulfill the command: "Do this in remembrance of me" is precisely the power of the promised Holy Spirit who alone, we might add, can realize and reactivate the saving significance of Jesus' words and deeds (see John 14:26). No wonder, then, that in the language of our Eucharistic Prayers, the logic of our commemoration of Christ leads inexorably to a petition, a clause in which we ask God to send or pour the Holy Spirit upon us and the gifts of bread and wine over which we give thanks and praise.

Interestingly, one contemporary example of the *anamnesis/epiclesis* section of a Eucharistic Prayer alludes directly to Augustine's theme of the realizing of the worshipping body as the "Body of Christ," and explicitly asks God to send the Holy Spirit "that we who receive Christ's body may indeed be the body of Christ" (*A New Zealand Prayer Book,* 1989, p. 487). This phrasing neatly summarizes the last two sections of our argument, and points us to the conclusion that it is through our participation in the celebration of the liturgy that we can be formed into Christ's Body, and shaped to reveal his likeness. In the scholastic terms of the medieval sacramental theologians, what we are alluding to is the *res tantum* (to distinguish it from the *res et sacramentum,* denoting the transformation of the eucharistic bread and wine into the body and blood of Christ), the final effect of our sharing in Communion, which can be nothing less than our transformation.

In conclusion we can say that the sacred space in which our sacramental celebrations are ritually enacted and embodied is, to use the poet R. S. Thomas' wondrous expression, "the laboratory of the Spirit." For although we, the worshippers, physically act out our worship through our bodily movement, posture and the physical acts of voicing words in the prayers, readings and song, we are also being "acted upon." Whether or not ritual in itself can do anything, or actually change its participants is a contested point in the field of ritual studies, but there are good grounds for saying that the practice of ritual seems to dispose its participants to the possibility of being changed. And on this basis, we invoke the doyen of ritual anthropology, Victor Turner, who insisted that the effects of ritual acts occur in the subjunctive mood. Catherine Bell (1989, p. 35) in her studies of the effect of ritual elucidates this understanding further, suggesting that the very practice of ritual orients and opens us to receive from the Other. It is not that the ritual conjures and channels the invoked presence, as if by magic, but that the practice of ritual places its participants precisely where they need to be if they are to receive and be shaped by that presence. Significantly, in her analysis of the dynamics of ritual action, Bell employs the formational vocabulary of "participation" and "impress," and draws the conclusion that "the schemes established by ritualization are impressed upon the participants as deriving from a reality beyond the activities of the group." What is done ritually in baptism and Eucharist should not be the creative design or intention of a single worship group, but should follow the pattern of what is "given" in the *tradition,* that dynamic handing over of what has been received: "I received from the Lord what I also delivered to you" (1 Corinthians 11:23). Ordinary things, such as bread for breaking and water for washing, are taken, but note, taken out of their ordinary use and context (the Eucharist is not, as is often suggested, meant to be a *meal* and baptism not literally a *bath!*), and used for a specific ritual purpose: "Do this in memory of me . . .;" Baptize in the name of the Father, Son and Holy Spirit." To draw on Catherine Bell's work again (1997," Chapter 7), ritual, though employed strategically, cannot be reduced to an instrumental mechanism whose effects are guaranteed simply by its performance (as though it happened solely in an automatic, *ex opere operatum* way), but is deeply embedded in the sedimented context of a historic community's values, beliefs, assumptions and practices. In other words, in performing the rite we actively draw on our cultural memory, we remember who we are and to whom we belong, as members of Christ's Body, the Church. This, of course, helps us to see the difference between a symbolic act of ritualization, such as the placing of flowers at the site of a fatal accident, and a "sacrament." For although all ritual actions might in some sense be sacramental, what constitutes a particular sacrament is the fact that it is the ritual action of the historically ordered, social body of the Church, and one that is legitimated by its appeal and reference to Jesus Christ. In terms of classical sacramental theology, this is precisely what is meant by Christ "instituting the sacraments," and following this logic, we could say that the imperatives: "Baptize!" and "Do this!" represent the signature of Christ, underwriting the ritual action with the promise of the presence and action of the triune God.

So, in terms of the repeated ritual action of sacramental celebration, it is Christ who is the (hidden) agent of the action, and the operation is none other than the working of the creative and recreative Spirit of God. It is Christ who calls worshippers and draws them together in his single offering to the Father, and through Communion seeks to indwell us bodily. But it is the transforming Holy Spirit who shapes our mortal and mutable bodies into the likeness of Christ. The human body in its corporeal materiality is formed in the womb, but aligned with the form of Christ once for all in baptism, realigned through repentance, and finally transformed into a spiritual body. But these are not distinct, or progressive phases, as if they were successive developmental stages of Christian growth, with the final hope being projected into a distant and unimaginable future. No, the process happens now, in the present and pregnant moment of worship. For in the liturgical act, time, we might say, concertinas, as the past impinges on the present, and the present opens up to the promised future. This is the basic meaning of *anamnesis,* of the biblical festivals of "memorial sacrifices." At the celebration of the Passover, a memorial feast commemorating the escape of the Hebrews from their bondage in Egypt, each Jew is told in the Mishnah that they are to imagine that they themselves were liberated from the bondage and oppression of Egypt (see also Deuteronomy 5:3 and Exodus 1:8). In this memorial feast the past informs the present time in a way which opens up and activates the promise, a new life of freedom and joy in a new land, "flowing with milk and honey." Likewise, in the anamnetic affirmation of faith in the celebration of the Christian Eucharist: "Christ, has died, Christ is risen, Christ will come again," time is condensed in the *kairos,* the moment of God's acting in and through the Spirit, in and through the occasion of worship. It is in this sense that the Christian is caught in the eschatological tension of "even now" and the "not yet" of our transformation. Perhaps we could even say that it is the pressure, as it were, of being caught between the "now," and the "not yet" which renews in us the *imago Dei* and shapes us more perfectly into the likeness of Christ. Furthermore, as we are being thus fashioned, Christ is literally bodied forth for others as we present "our bodies as a living sacrifice" (Romans 12:1), and at this point liturgy shades into ethics, and worship into the variegated pattern of our relationships and occupations.

7
Epilogue: Images of Formation

It is often said that the face is the most expressive part of human anatomy, but for the French sculptor, Auguste Rodin, a person's hands were equally expressive of the human person. When we look at examples of his work, such as the *Burghers of Calais* (1886–1888), we can see how he sculpted the hands of his figures to convey their mood and character. The two pieces of his oeuvre that I want to reflect on use hands to extraordinary effect—a late piece entitled *The Cathedral* (1908) and the *Hand of God* (1898). Both these sculpted pieces are eloquent images of formation, of meeting and making. *The Cathedral* (reproduced on the front cover of this book) is simply the meeting of two hands, and evokes the work of the great Michelangelo, whose genius so inspired Rodin at the time when he was developing his own vigorous realistic artistic style. The rendering of the two hands combines and expresses both strength and tenderness, and like Michelangelo's painting of the hand of God and Adam on the ceiling of the Sistine Chapel is charged with extraordinary power. The two opened hands are drawn together, but do not quite meet, evoking the response and movement of desire, of one to another. The sculpture is a strong and sensitive piece and recalls the imagery of Irenaeus, the second-century Bishop of Lyons, who writing of God's work of creation and redemption repeatedly spoke of Christ and the Holy Spirit, the Word and Wisdom of God, as being the two hands of God. Irenaeus, arguing against the Gnostics who denied any direct involvement of the Creator God with the stuff of creation, adopted the biblical imagery of our being fashioned by God's hands (Job 10:8; cf. Psalm 119:73) to celebrate the intimate involvement of the triune God in the shaping of his creation and in forming us according to the pattern of his Son, the true image of the invisible God: for we are "formed after the likeness of God and molded by his hands" (*Against the Heresies* IV.4). 137

One might expect that a sculpted piece entitled *The Cathedral* would have shown two hands raised together in a gesture of prayer, but this is not what Rodin's depicts. What we have here is not the coming together of a person's left and right hand, but in fact two sculptured right hands, meeting to form a concave space. It is a hand meeting the hand of another, creating a defined and yet open space. The very composition and its title evokes the Hebrew image of the tabernacle, literally a covering, which defines a place of meeting and encounter with the holy Other and invites us to see "the cathedral," or any other sacred space, as essentially a place of meeting in which we come together with others, and together encounter the sacred Other, who promises to come and dwell with and among us. The fact that the hands, though powerfully drawn together, do not actually meet reminds us that when we literally open our hands and reach out towards the other (whether the other is another person or God), that "other" is always different from ourselves, and to some extent always remains a stranger to us. For it is the very difference of the other which draws us and leads us deeper into the mystery of a presence we can never fully comprehend, let alone possess. Correspondingly, our places of worship should never be enclosed and confined spaces, but sufficiently open and expansive as to signal the presence of the God who is greater than we might think and imagine, and yet draws us into communion with himself.

Rodin's earlier sculpture *The Hand of God* (1898) is simply exquisite, and was derived from a sculptured piece of the right hand of Pierre de Wiessant that he began in 1884 and worked and reworked on a number of separate occasions. The shaping of a sculpture was labor intensive. Rodin, we are told, modeled clay with the intensity of flesh, and only when he was satisfied with the clay figure would it be rendered in plaster for a bronze cast, or used as a model for a marble or stone sculpture. The final form of *The Hand of God* is wonderfully wrought and emerges from the rough textured block of marble. The two exquisite and polished human forms, one male and the other female, emerge from the rough hewn marble and almost tumble out of God's right hand at one and the same time. Remember, indeed, the rock from which you were hewn (Isaiah 51:1).

Rodin expressly wanted to respect the material with which he worked, and characteristically retained some of the natural material that he sculpted as being integral to the final piece. This was why critics and commentators derided his work as "partial sculptures" and castigated him for his unfinished workmanship. He had admired the finely finished and monumental figures of Michelangelo in San Lorenzo, Florence, but Rodin had first learned his art by contemplating the fragments of classic antique sculpture displayed in the Louvre in Paris. He did not aim to render the perfect human figure, so admired by the neoclassicists, but to intimate the vitality of natural, living forms, and in the final piece to indicate that the shaping of a concealed and hidden form was a labored process. For Rodin, the creative process invariably began with the shaping of his chosen material, clay, recalling for us the primal biblical image of God shaping Adam from the stuff of the earth. This biblical image recurs in the writing of the prophet Isaiah, who comforts a displaced and dispossessed people by recalling that as it was God who first shaped them as his people, they remained his people in whatever circumstances they found themselves (see Isaiah 43:1; 44.2–3; 45:1–12). Even when all was destruction and ruin and the people were disfigured by their sin and disobedience, the prophet's lament could confidently voice the conviction that their destiny was in God's hands: "Yet, O Lord, you are our Father; we are the clay, and you are the potter" (Isaiah 64:8). The identity conferred upon Israel as God's people was indelibly stamped upon them, and as Jeremiah was led to see, the God who had so shaped them could reshape them as a potter remolds a disfigured pot:

> I went down to the potter's house, and there he was working at his wheel. And the vessel he was making of clay was spoiled in the potter's hand, and he reworked it into another vessel as it seemed good to him. Then the word of the Lord came to me. "O house of Israel, can I not do to you as this potter has done? Says the Lord. Behold, like the clay in the potter's hand, so are you in my hand, O house of Israel" (Jeremiah 18:3–6).

Although far from being a conventional practicing Catholic, Rodin was a person of marked religious sensibilities and when once asked whether he believed in God, replied that he believed in God because it was God who had invented modeling. The Old Testament image of God as a potter is appropriated by Paul in Romans 9, a passage in which he draws out the lines of continuity between the Christian community and Israel as a people shaped by the hands of God. As Theodore of Mopsuestia impressed upon the newly baptized, in repeatedly speaking of the effect of sacramental grace in shaping, recasting and remolding us, Christians are to be like moist yielding clay in the hand of the potter.

In the early 1870s, while Rodin was away from Paris working in Brussels, his partner Rose Beuret was entrusted with looking after the sculptured clay models in his studio, and in his letters, Rodin frequently reminded her to keep the clay moist and to cover them with damp cloths or papers. The unfinished work had to remain malleable, otherwise it would crack and break apart. But what of ourselves as "God's workmanship"; how are we to remain moist in God's hand? The rich symbolic world of liturgy points us to acts of penitence and the remembrance of baptism as occasions when we might yield ourselves to God's gently shaping hands. For all of us there will be times when we shed tears for ourselves and for others. There might also be the occasional tears of repentance, and in a penitential rite, the ritual of sprinkling of water of absolution. In some religious communities, the abbot walks around the members at the end of Compline (the night service before the Community retires to rest and sleep), silently sprinkling each in turn. In the Ambrosian liturgical tradition there is a memorial of baptism at the end of Sunday Vespers, and this practice can be extended by providing a bowl of baptismal water from the font at the entrance to the church, which we might take with two fingers and thumb and make the sign of the cross as we enter and leave the church building. This ancient custom provides a continual reminder of the waters of baptism which is, as Theodore of Mopsuestia suggests, the amniotic fluid of the womb of mother Church and the very spring of our Christian life:

> [In] the mother's womb it is God's hand that forms us according to his design . . . in baptism the water becomes a womb [and there] it is the grace of the Spirit which forms him there for a second birth and makes him a completely new person (*Baptismal Homily* II).

Baptism is a once-and-for-all event, but we constantly need to ask for the dew of God's mercy if we are not to become too rigid in our outlook, so hardened in our attitudes that we resist the imprint of Christ's fingers, forming us from his image into his very likeness. At this point in our reflection we might consider again Rodin's *Hand of God,* and now imagine Irenaeus' second hand, that is, the invisible hand of God's Spirit, which seeks to shape us into the likeness of Christ (*Against the Heresies* V.6.1). As we contemplate Rodin's *Hand of God* we might imagine that second hand gently drawing out and making visible our true form, the very likeness of Christ.

So again, our reflections return us to pneumatology, to our understanding of the person and work of the Holy Spirit. In the prophetic oracle in Isaiah 44:1–3, a direct link is made between the "Spirit" and "formation" of God's people, and in the apocryphal Book of Judith the terms are brought into closest relationship in a song praising God's creativity: "You did send forth your Spirit, and it formed them" (Judith 16:14b). As the Spirit is the spirit of formation, so it is this work of formation that is the primary act of God the Holy Spirit in the embodied enactment of our sacramental celebrations.

No wonder, then, that we must eagerly and earnestly pray that the Spirit may "form us into the likeness of Christ." For the hand of God's Word, which impresses the very divine image upon us at baptism, is complemented by the other hand of God's Wisdom, which both leads and draws out from us, through the embodied ritual acts of repentance and Communion, the very likeness of Christ. And why? Because, as the poet tells us, it is the Father's good purpose that Christ should play

> . . . in ten thousand places,
> Lovely in limbs, and lovely in eyes not his
> To the Father through the features of men's faces.

Gerard Manley Hopkins,
"As Kingfishers Catch Fire"

Bibliography and Further Reading

Anderson, E. Byron, *Worship and Christian Identity: Practicing Ourselves,* The Liturgical Press, Collegeville, 2003

Balthasar, Hans Urs von, *Cosmic Liturgy: The Universe According to Maximus the Confessor,* trans. Brian E. Daley, SJ, Ignatius Press, San Francisco, 2003

Balthasar, Hans Urs von, *The Glory of the Lord: A Theological Aesthetics. Volume 1: Seeing the Form,* T. & T. Clark, Edinburgh, 1982

Barker, Margaret, *The Great High Priest: The Temple Roots of Christian Liturgy,* T. & T. Clark, London, 2003

Barth, Karl, *Church Dogmatics,* III.1: The Doctrine of Creation, T. & T. Clark, Edinburgh 1958

Bell, Catherine, *Ritual: Perspectives and Dimensions,* Oxford University Press, Oxford, 1997

Bell, Catherine, "Ritual Change and Changing Rituals," *Worship,* Volume 63, 1989

Bell, Clive, *Art,* Chatto & Windus, London, 1914

Boldovin, John, Rule of Prayer, *Rule of Faith: Essays in Honor of Aidan Kavanagh,* Pueblo, New York, 1996

Bradshaw, Paul F., *Eucharistic Origins,* SPCK, London, 2004

Brown, David and Loades, Ann (eds), *Christ: The Sacramental Word, Incarnation, Sacrament and Poetry,* SPCK, London, 1996

Brown, Peter, *The Body and Society: Men, Women and Sexual Renunciation in Early Christianity,* Faber & Faber, London, 1988

Brueggemann, Walter, *Theology of the Old Testament,* Fortress Press, Minneapolis, 1997

Butler, Ruth, *Rodin: The Shape of Genius,* Yale University Press, New Haven, 1993

Chauvet, Louis-Marie and Kabasele, Francois (eds), "Liturgy and the Body", *Concilium 3,* Lumbala, 1995

Chauvet, Louis-Marie, *Symbol and Sacrament,* The Liturgical Press, Collegeville, 1995

Chauvet, Louis-Marie, *The Sacraments: The Word of God at the Mercy of the Body,* The Liturgical Press, Collegeville, 1997

Clement, Olivier, *The Roots of Christian Mysticism: Text and Commentary,* New City, London, 1993

Clement, Olivier, *On Human Being: A Spiritual Anthropology,* New City, London, 2000

Coakley, Sarah (ed.), *Religion and the Body,* Cambridge University Press, Cambridge, 1997

Davies, Oliver, *The Creativity of God, World, Eucharist, Reason,* Cambridge University Press, Cambridge, 2004

Dawtry, Anne and Irvine, Christopher, *Art and Worship,* SPCK, London, 2002

Dix, Gregory, *The Shape of the Liturgy,* Dacre, London, 1945

Dunn, James D. G., *The Theology of Paul the Apostle,* T. & T. Clark, Edinburgh, 1998

Dunn, James D. G., *The Cambridge Companion to St Paul,* Cambridge University Press, Cambridge, 2003

FitzPatrick, P. J., *In Breaking of Bread: The Eucharist and Ritual,* Cambridge University Press, Cambridge, 1993

Fee, Gordon, *Paul's Letter to the Philippians,* Eerdmans, Grand Rapids, 1995

Fisch, T. (ed.), *Liturgy and Tradition: Theological Reflections of Alexander Schmemann,* St. Vladimir's Press, New York, 1990

Ford, David, *Self and Salvation: Being Transformed,* Cambridge University Press, Cambridge, 1999

Garrigan, Siobhan, *Beyond Ritual: Sacramental Theology after Habermas,* Ashgate, Aldershot, 2004

Giddens, Anthony, *Modernity and Self-Identity: Self and Society in Late Modern Age,* Polity Press, Cambridge, 1991

Hooker, Morna, *From Adam to Christ: Essays on Paul,* Cambridge University Press, Cambridge, 1990

Hughes, Graham, *Worship as Meaning: A Liturgical Theology for Late Modernity,* Cambridge University Press, Cambridge, 2003

Irvine, Christopher, *Worship, Church and Society,* Canterbury Press, Norwich, 1993

Jennings, Theodore, "On Ritual Knowledge," *Journal of Religion,* Volume 62, Number 2, April 1982

Johnson, Maxwell E., *The Rites of Christian Initiation: Their Evolution and Interpretation,* The Liturgical Press, Collegeville, 1999

Johnson, Maxwell E., T*he Documents of Baptismal Liturgy,* SPCK, London, 2003

Karkkainen, Veli-Matti, *Towards A Pneumatological Theology,* ed. Amos Young, University Press of America, Lanham, 2002

Kavanagh, Aidan, "Seeing Liturgically," in *Time and Community,* ed. J. Neil Alexander, Pastoral Press, Portland, 1990

Kerr, Fergus, *Theology after Wittgenstein,* Basil Blackwell, Oxford, 1986

Kilmartin, Edward, *The Eucharist in the West: History and Theology,* The Liturgical Press, Collegeville, 1998

Klee, Felix (ed.), *The Diaries of Paul Klee, 1898–1918,* University of California Press, Berkeley, 1964

Kuschel, Karl-Josef, *The Poet as Mirror: Human Nature, God and Jesus in Twentieth-Century Literature,* SCM Press, London, 1999

Ladner, Gerhardt B., *God, Cosmos and Humankind: The World of Early Christian Symbolism,* University of California, Berkeley, 1995

Langer, Susanne K., *Feeling and Form: A Theory of Art,* Charles Scribner's Sons, New York, 1953

Lathrop, Gordon W., *Holy Things: A Liturgical Ecclesiology,* Fortress Press, Minneapolis, 1993

Lee, Dorothy, *Transfiguration,* Continuum, London, 2004

Lopera, Jose Alvarez (ed.), *El Greco: Identity and Transformation,* Museo Thyssen Bornemisza, Madrid, 1999

Lossky, Vladimir, *In the Image and Likeness of God,* St Vladimir's Seminary Press, Crestwood, New York, 1974

McFadyen, Alistair, *The Call to Personhood: A Christian Theory of the Individual in Social Relationships,* Cambridge University Press, Cambridge, 1990

Meyendorff, John, *A Study of Gregory Palamas,* St Vladimir's Seminary Press, Crestwood, New York, 1998

Moltmann-Wendel, Elisabeth, *I am My Body,* SCM Press, London, 1994

Nichols, Bridget, *Liturgical Hermeneutics: Interpreting Liturgical Rites in Performance,* Peter Lang, Frankfurt am Main, 1996

Nichols, Bridget and McGregor, Alistair, *The Eucharistic Epiclesis,* Ushaw Library Publications, Durham, 2002

Pecklers, Keith, *Liturgy in a Postmodern World,* Continuum, London, 2003

Pettersen, Alvyn, *Athanasius and the Human Body,* The Bristol Press, Bristol, 1990

Porter, Roy, *Flesh in the Age of Reason,* Allen Lane, London, 2003

Power, David N., *The Eucharistic Mystery: Revitalizing the Tradition,* Gill & Macmillan, Dublin, 1992

Ricoeur, Paul, *Hermeneutics and the Human Sciences,* ed. and trans. John B. Thompson, Cambridge University Press, Cambridge, 1981

Ricoeur, Paul, *Oneself as Another,* trans. Kathleen Blamey, University of Chicago Press, Chicago, 1994

Russell, Norman, *The Doctrine of Deification in the Greek Patristic Tradition,* Oxford University Press, Oxford, 2004

Schiller, Gertrud, *Iconography of Christian Art,* Volume 1, trans. J. Seligman, Lund Humphries, London, 1971

Segal, A. F., *Paul the Convert,* Yale University Press, New Haven, 1990

Stevenson, Kenneth, *Handing On: Borderlands of Worship and Tradition,* London, Darton, Longman & Todd, 1996

Steiner, George, *Real Presences,* University of Chicago Press, Chicago, 1991

Taylor, Charles, *Sources of the Self: The Making of the Modern Identity,* Cambridge University Press, Cambridge, 1989

Torevell, David, *Losing the Sacred: Ritual, Modernity and Liturgical Reform,* T. & T. Clark, London, 2000

Watson, J. R., *The English Hymn: A Critical and Historical Study,* Clarendon, Oxford, 1997

Whalen, Robert, *The Poetry of Immanence: Sacrament in Donne and Herbert,* University of Toronto Press, Toronto, 2002

Whaling, Frank, J., *John and Charles Wesley* (Classics of Western Spirituality), SPCK, London, 1981

Wharton, A. J., "Ritual and Reconstructed Meaning: The Neonian Baptistery in Ravenna," *Art Bulletin,* Volume LXIX, Number 1, 1987

Yarnold, E., *The Awe Inspiring Rites of Initiation,* T. & T. Clark, Edinburgh, 1994 Young, Frances and Ford, David, *Meaning and Truth in 2 Corinthians,* SPCK, London, 1997

Ziesler, John, *Pauline Christianity,* Oxford, Oxford University Press, 1988

Index